from the staff

appliqué has come a long way from its more traditional hand-stitched beginnings. Most notably, sewing machines with built-in decorative stitches and fusible web for adhering shapes to foundation fabric have allowed quilters to achieve appliquéd results in a shorter time. And while hand appliqué still thrives in popularity, new technology has opened the doors to those with limited free time but who still crave the look of traditional appliqué.

Regardless of your skill level, you'll find the step-by-step instructions and easy-to-follow photos in the Appliqué Primer invaluable references for completing your machine-appliqué projects. From preparing the appliqué pieces to different methods of stitching the appliqués to foundation fabric, you'll find in the primer everything you need for success.

Whatever your ability, you'll find a quilting project to suit your décor or any gift-giving occasion. Re-create the projects exactly as shown—or create your own unique color palette for a custom look. We hope you will be pleased with the results and will find that machine appliqué is a skill you'll put to use frequently as you progress on your quilting journey.

enjoy!

table of contents

fusible-web appliqué

Use today's technology to simplify handling your appliqué shapes. With a piece of fusible web and a warm iron, you can easily hold your appliqué pieces in position prior to stitching.

butterfly linens

As cheerful as a summer day, these bands of machine-appliquéd butterflies and flowers will brighten the plainest of sheet sets.

Designer: Diane Hansen
Photographer: Scott Little

materials

⅛ yard of green pin dot for appliqués
⅛ yard of green stripe for appliqués
Scraps of assorted yellow, pink, orange, red, teal, blue, and purple prints for appliqués
Embroidery floss to match the appliqués
Twin flat sheet
Two standard pillowcases
Machine embroidery thread in matching colors
1 yard of lightweight fusible web

FINISHED SHEET: 64×100"
FINISHED PILLOWCASE: 20×30"

These appliqués were made for a twin-size sheet and standard pillowcases. Make more or fewer appliqués depending upon the width of your sheet and size of your pillowcases.

cut the fabrics

To make the best use of your fabrics, cut the pieces in the order that follows. The patterns are on *this page* and *page 5*.

To use fusible web for appliquéing, as was done in this project, complete the following steps.

1. Lay the fusible web paper side up over the patterns. Use a pencil to trace each pattern the number of times indicated, leaving ½" between tracings. Cut out each piece roughly ¼" outside the traced lines.

2. Following the manufacturer's instructions, press the fusible-web shapes onto the wrong sides of the designated fabrics; let cool. Cut out the fabric shapes on the drawn lines. Peel off the paper backings.

From green pin dot, cut:
● 4 *each* of patterns F, K, L, and M
From green stripe, cut:
● 4 *each* of patterns I and J
From assorted yellow, pink, orange, red, teal, blue, and purple print scraps, cut:
● 8 *each* of patterns N and H
● 8 sets of 7 of Pattern G
● 5 *each* of patterns A, B, C, D, and E

appliqué the sheet and pillowcases

1. Referring to the Applique Placement diagrams *below* and *opposite*, and the photographs at *right* and on *page 3* for placement, position the prepared appliqué pieces on the pillowcases and flat sheet; fuse in place.

2. Machine-satin-stitch around each of the appliqué shapes to complete the sheet set. Use a smaller satin-stitch to create the butterfly antennae.

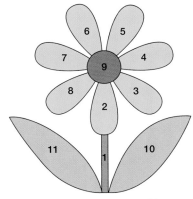

Daisy Appliqué Placement Diagram
(numbers on diagrams indicate sewing sequence)

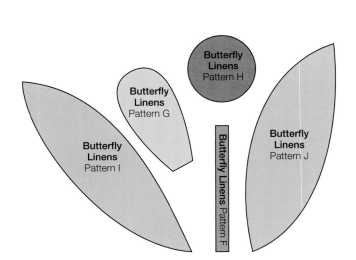

Full-Size Patterns

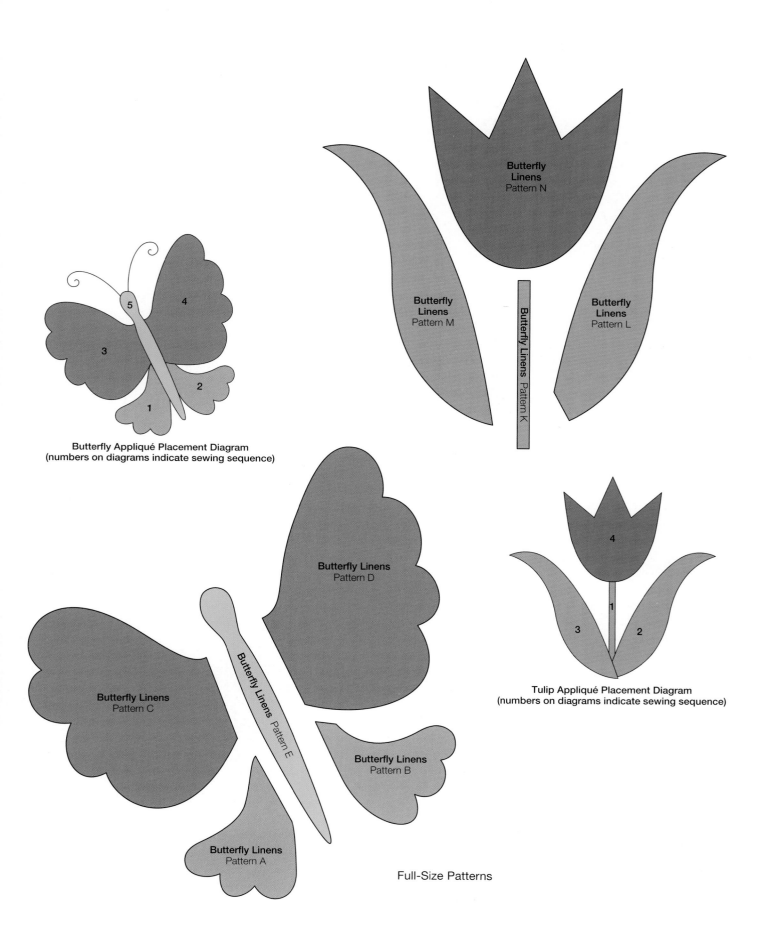

Butterfly Linens
Pattern N

Butterfly Linens
Pattern M

Butterfly Linens Pattern K

Butterfly Linens
Pattern L

Butterfly Appliqué Placement Diagram
(numbers on diagrams indicate sewing sequence)

Butterfly Linens
Pattern D

Butterfly Linens Pattern E

Tulip Appliqué Placement Diagram
(numbers on diagrams indicate sewing sequence)

Butterfly Linens
Pattern C

Butterfly Linens
Pattern B

Butterfly Linens
Pattern A

Full-Size Patterns

abstract whimsy

Piece the simple square background of this quilt for a foundation of oversized, appliquéd shapes.

Designer: Jenni Paige   Photographer: Perry Struse

materials
- 10—⅓-yard pieces of assorted orange, red, and gold prints for blocks
- 10—⅓-yard pieces of assorted dark purple, green, and teal prints for outer border
- ½ yard of wavy red print for inner border
- ⅝ yard of wavy green print for binding
- ⅔ yard of gold print for star and swirl appliqués
- ⅓ yard of dark green print for leaf appliqués
- ⅓ yard of light green print for leaf appliqués
- 3¾ yards of backing fabric
- 67×77" of quilt batting
- 3 yards of lightweight fusible web

FINISHED BLOCK: 9½" square
FINISHED QUILT TOP: 61×70½"

Quantities specified for 44/45"-wide, 100% cotton fabrics. All measurements include a ¼" seam allowance. Sew with right sides together unless otherwise stated.

cut the fabrics
To make the best use of your fabrics, cut the pieces in the order that follows.

From assorted orange, red, and gold prints, cut:
- 20—10" squares

From assorted dark purple, green, and teal prints, cut:
- 8—10×12" rectangles
- 14—10" squares

From wavy red print, cut:
- 5—2½×42" strips for inner border

From wavy green print, cut:
- 7—2½×42" binding strips

assemble the quilt center
1. Referring to the photograph, *opposite*, for placement, lay out the 20 orange, red, and gold print 10" squares in five rows of four squares each. Sew together the squares in each row. Press the seam allowances in one direction, alternating the direction with each row.

2. Join the rows to make the quilt center. Press the seam allowances in one direction. The pieced quilt center should measure 38½×48", including the seam allowances.

add the borders
1. Cut and piece the red wavy print 2½×42" strips to make the following:
- 2—2½×53" inner border strips
- 2—2½×43" inner border strips

2. Add a short wavy red print inner border strip to the top edge of the pieced quilt center, matching the center of the strip and the center of the quilt edge. Sew together, beginning and ending the seam ¼" from the quilt-top corners (see Diagram 1, *above right*). Allow excess border fabric to extend beyond the edges. Repeat with the remaining short wavy red print inner border strip on the bottom edge and the long wavy red print inner border strips on the side edges. Press the seam allowances toward the border strips.

Diagram 1

3. At one corner, lap one border strip over the other (see Diagram 2). Align the edge of a 90° right triangle with the raw edge of the top strip so the long edge of the triangle intersects the seams and the corner. With a pencil, draw along the edge of the triangle from the seams out to the raw edge. Place the bottom border strip on top and repeat the marking process.

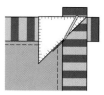
Diagram 2

4. With the right sides of adjacent border strips together, match the marked seam lines and pin (see Diagram 3).

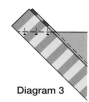
Diagram 3

5. Beginning with a backstitch at the quilt top edge, sew together the strips, stitching exactly on the marked lines to the outside of the border strips. Check the right side to see that the corner lies flat.

Trim the excess fabric, leaving ¼" seam allowances. Press the seam allowance open. Mark and sew the remaining corners in the same manner.

6. Referring to the photograph on *page 6* for color placement, sew together two of the assorted dark purple, green, and teal print 10" squares and two assorted dark purple, green, and teal print 10×12" rectangles to make the pieced top border. Repeat to make a pieced bottom border. Sew the pieced borders to the top and bottom edges of the quilt center. Press all seam allowances toward the inner border.

7. Sew together five dark purple, green, and teal print 10" squares and two dark purple, green, and teal print 10×12" rectangles to make a pieced side border. Repeat to make a second pieced side border. Sew the pieced side borders to the side edges of the quilt center to complete the quilt top. Press all seam allowances toward the inner border.

appliqué the quilt top

The patterns are on *pages 8–11*. To make templates of the patterns, follow the instructions in Appliqué Primer, which begins on *page 82*. To use fusible web for appliquéing, as was done in this project, complete the following steps.

1. Lay the fusible web, paper side up, over the patterns. Use a pencil to trace each pattern piece the number of times indicated, leaving ½" between tracings. Cut out each piece roughly ¼" outside the traced lines.

2. Following the manufacturer's instructions, press the fusible-web shapes onto the wrong sides of the designated fabrics; let cool. Cut out the fabric shapes on the drawn lines. Peel off the paper backings.

From gold print, cut:
● 3 of Pattern A
● 4 of Pattern B
From dark green print, cut:
● 5 of Pattern C
From light green print, cut:
● 5 of Pattern D

3. Referring to the photograph on *page 6* for placement, position the appliqué shapes on the quilt, layering the leaf shapes as needed. When the appliqué shapes are in the desired position, fuse in place.

4. Using matching thread, machine-appliqué the shapes in place.

complete the quilt

1. Layer the quilt top, batting, and backing according to the instructions in Quilting Basics, which begins on *page 94*. Quilt as desired.

2. Use the wavy green print 2½"-wide strips to bind the quilt according to the instructions in Quilting Basics.

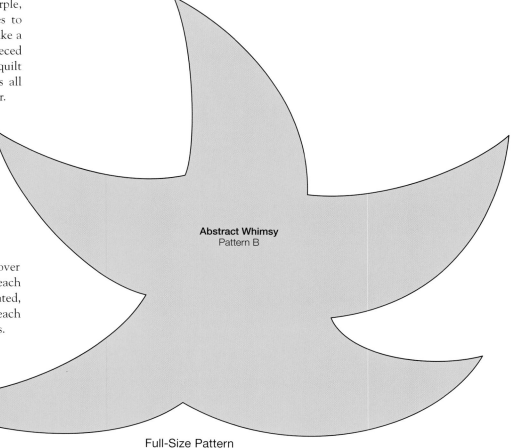

Abstract Whimsy
Pattern B

Full-Size Pattern

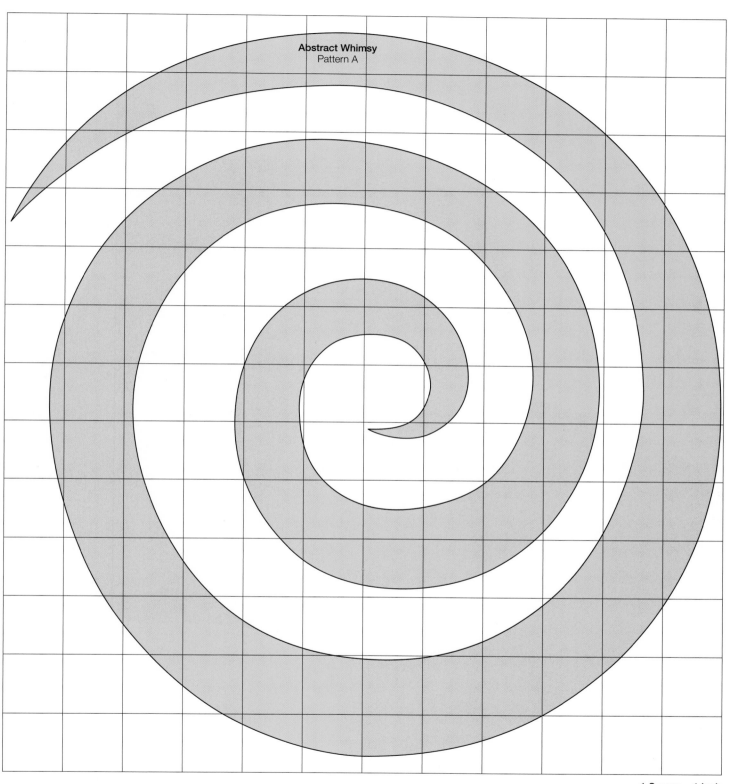

Abstract Whimsy
Pattern A

1 Square = 1 Inch
Enlarge @ 160%

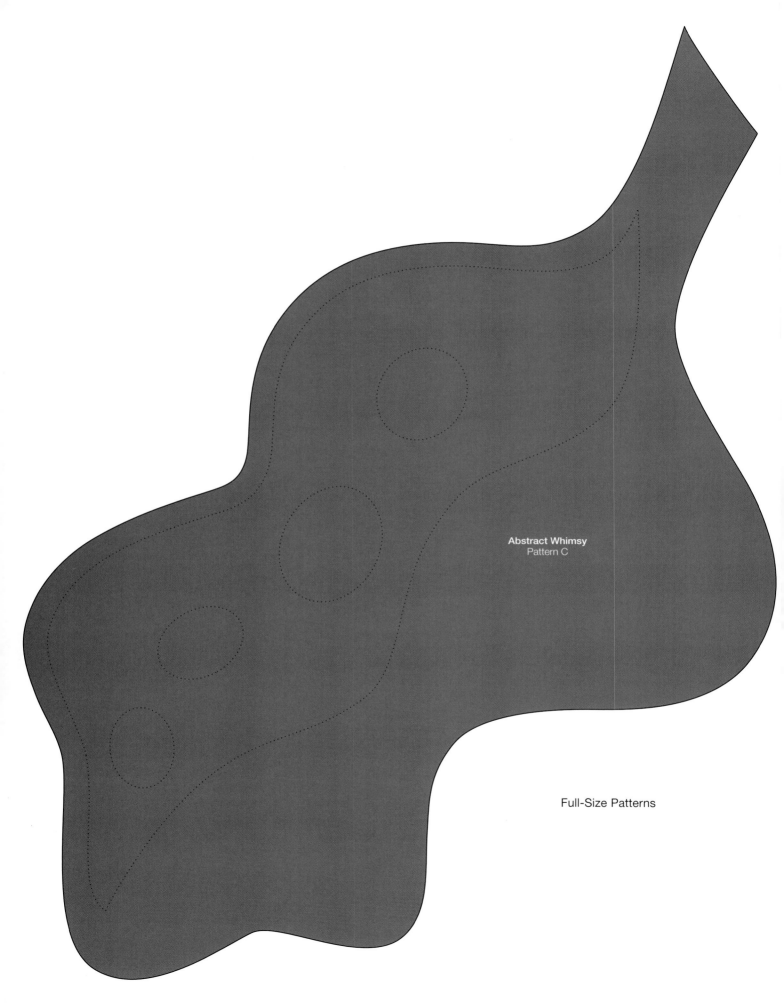

Abstract Whimsy
Pattern C

Full-Size Patterns

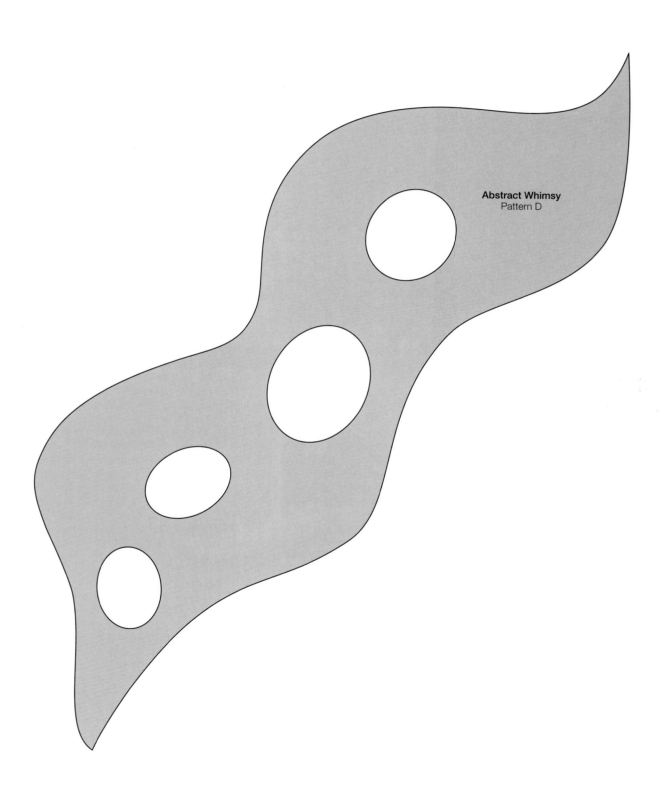

Abstract Whimsy
Pattern D

Hang on to the memories of a warm summer day with a machine-appliquéd garden of flowers stitched to last for years. Finish it with a pieced hourglass border to set off your handiwork.

Designer: Pat Sloan
Photographer: Perry Struse

hollyhock
delight

materials

14½×20½" piece of cream print for appliqué foundation

6" square of light yellow print for sun center appliqué

7" square of yellow print for flower center and sun appliqués

10" square of gold print for beehive appliqués

7" square of dark gold print for sun appliqué

⅛ yard of blue floral for inner border

¼ yard of blue print for pieced border

½ yard of dark blue print for pieced border and binding

10" square of blue polka dot for flower appliqués

12" square of dark green print for stem and beehive door appliqués

11" square of light green print for leaf and stem appliqués

2×4" piece of green print for dragonfly appliqué

4×6" piece of rose floral for dragonfly wing appliqués

⅛ yard of red print for hollyhock appliqués

⅛ yard of red floral for hollyhock appliqués

⅛ yard of multicolor stripe for hollyhock appliqués

5—8" squares of assorted light prints for hollyhock center appliqués

¾ yard of backing fabric

27×33" of quilt batting

1 yard of lightweight fusible web

FINISHED QUILT TOP: 21×27"

Quantities specified for 44/45"-wide, 100% cotton fabrics. All measurements include a ¼" seam allowance. Sew with right sides together unless otherwise stated.

cut the fabrics

To make the best use of your fabrics, cut the pieces in the order that follows. The patterns are on *pages 15–17.* To use fusible web for appliquéing, as was done in this project, complete the following steps.

1. Lay the fusible web, paper side up, over the patterns. Use a pencil to trace each pattern the number of times indicated, leaving ½" between tracings. Cut out each piece roughly ¼" outside the traced lines.

2. Following the manufacturer's instructions, press the fusible-web shapes onto the wrong sides of the designated fabrics; let cool. Cut out the fabric shapes on the drawn lines. Peel off the paper backings.

From light yellow print, cut:
● 1 of Pattern D

From yellow print, cut:
● 1 of Pattern E
● 4 of Pattern G

From gold print, cut:
● 1 *each* of patterns A and B

From dark gold print, cut:
● 1 of Pattern F

From blue floral, cut:
● 2—1×21½" inner border strips
● 2—1×14½" inner border strips

From blue print, cut:
● 14—4¼" squares, cutting each diagonally twice in an X for a total of 56 triangles

From dark blue print, cut:
● 3—2½×42" binding strips
● 14—4¼" squares, cutting each diagonally twice in an X for a total of 56 triangles

From blue polka dot, cut:
● 4 of Pattern H

From dark green print, cut:
● 1 *each* of patterns C and I

From light green print, cut:
● 1 *each* of patterns Q and R

From green print, cut:
● 1 of Pattern J

From rose floral, cut:
● 1 *each* of patterns K, K reversed, L, and L reversed

From red print, cut:
● 3 of Pattern M
● 2 each of patterns N and O

From red floral, cut:
● 2 of Pattern N
● 4 of Pattern O

From multicolor stripe, cut:
● 2 of Pattern M
● 3 of Pattern N
● 4 of Pattern O

From assorted light prints, cut:
● 5 of Pattern N
● 7 of Pattern O
● 10 of Pattern P

appliqué the sun

1. Referring to the Appliqué Placement Diagram on *page 14* and the photograph *opposite,* arrange appliqué pieces D, E, and F on the cream print 14½×20½" appliqué foundation. Fuse the appliqués in place.

2. Using threads in colors that match the fabrics, machine-blanket-stitch the edges of the shapes in place.

add the inner border

1. Sew the blue floral 1×14½" inner border strip to the top and bottom edges of the cream print 14½×20½" appliqué foundation.

2. Then join a blue floral 1×21½" inner border strip to each side edge of the cream print appliqué foundation. Press all seam allowances toward the inner border.

assemble and add the outer border

1. Referring to the Hourglass Unit Diagram, sew together two blue print triangles and two dark blue print triangles in pairs. Press the seam allowances toward the dark blue print triangles.

Hourglass Unit Diagram

2. Join the triangle pairs to make an hourglass unit. Press the seam allowances in one direction. The pieced hourglass unit should measure 3½" square, including the seam allowances.

3. Repeat steps 1 and 2 to make a total of 28 hourglass units.

4. Sew together five hourglass units to make a top pieced border strip. The pieced border strip should measure 3½×15½", including the seam allowances. Repeat to make a bottom pieced border strip. Sew the pieced border strips to the top and bottom edges of the quilt center. Press the seam allowances toward the blue floral inner border.

5. Sew together nine hourglass units to make a side pieced border strip. The pieced border strip should measure 3½×27½", including the seam allowances. Repeat to make a second side pieced border strip. Sew the pieced border strips to the side edges of the quilt center. Press the seam allowances toward the blue floral inner border.

appliqué the quilt top

1. Referring to the Appliqué Placement Diagram and the photograph on *page 12* for placement, arrange the appliqué pieces on the quilt top. Layer the pieces as needed and pin in place.

2. Cut and position small pieces of the dark green print for stems between the hollyhock flowers.

3. Remove the pins and fuse the appliqués in place.

4. Using matching thread, machine-blanket-stitch the edges of the shapes in place, working from the bottom layer to the top layer to complete the quilt top.

complete the quilt

1. Layer the quilt top, batting, and backing according to the instructions in Quilting Basics, which begins on *page 94*.

2. Quilt as desired. Designer Pat Sloan machine-quilted the blue print border hourglass units and the appliqué foundation in a freehand style and outlined around the appliqué pieces.

3. Use the dark blue print 2½×42" strips to bind the quilt according to the instructions in Quilting Basics.

Appliqué Placement Diagram

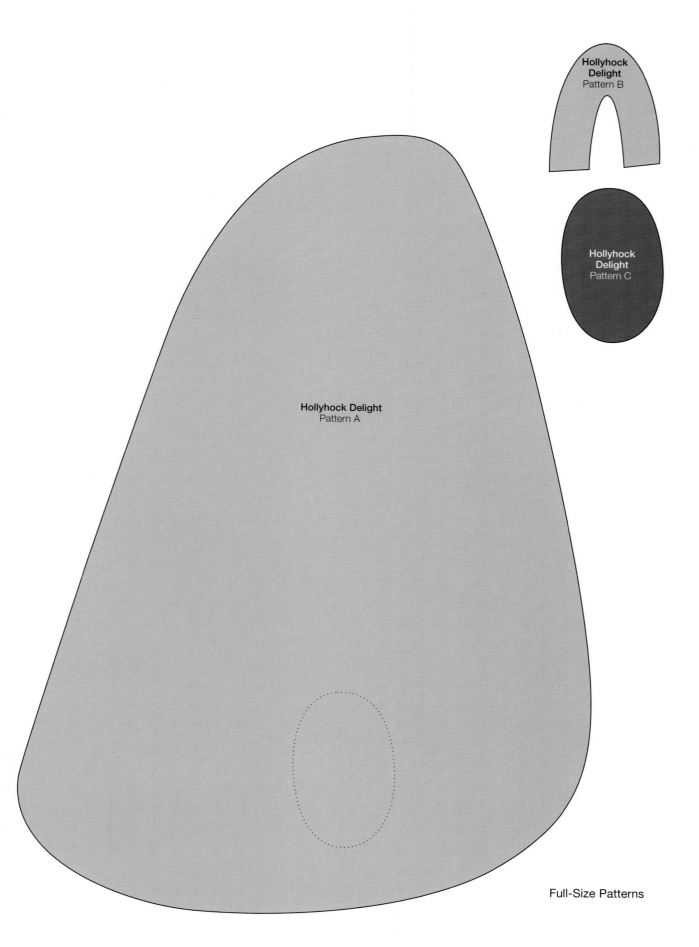

Hollyhock Delight
Pattern B

Hollyhock Delight
Pattern C

Hollyhock Delight
Pattern A

Full-Size Patterns

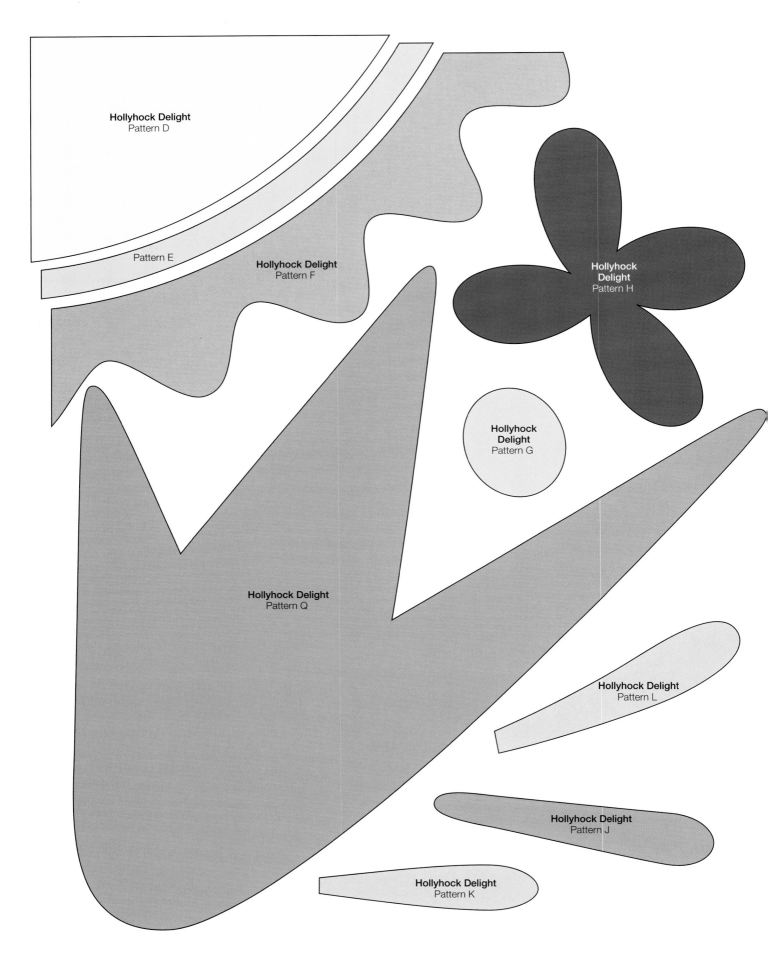

Hollyhock Delight
Pattern D

Pattern E

Hollyhock Delight
Pattern F

Hollyhock
Delight
Pattern H

Hollyhock
Delight
Pattern G

Hollyhock Delight
Pattern Q

Hollyhock Delight
Pattern L

Hollyhock Delight
Pattern J

Hollyhock Delight
Pattern K

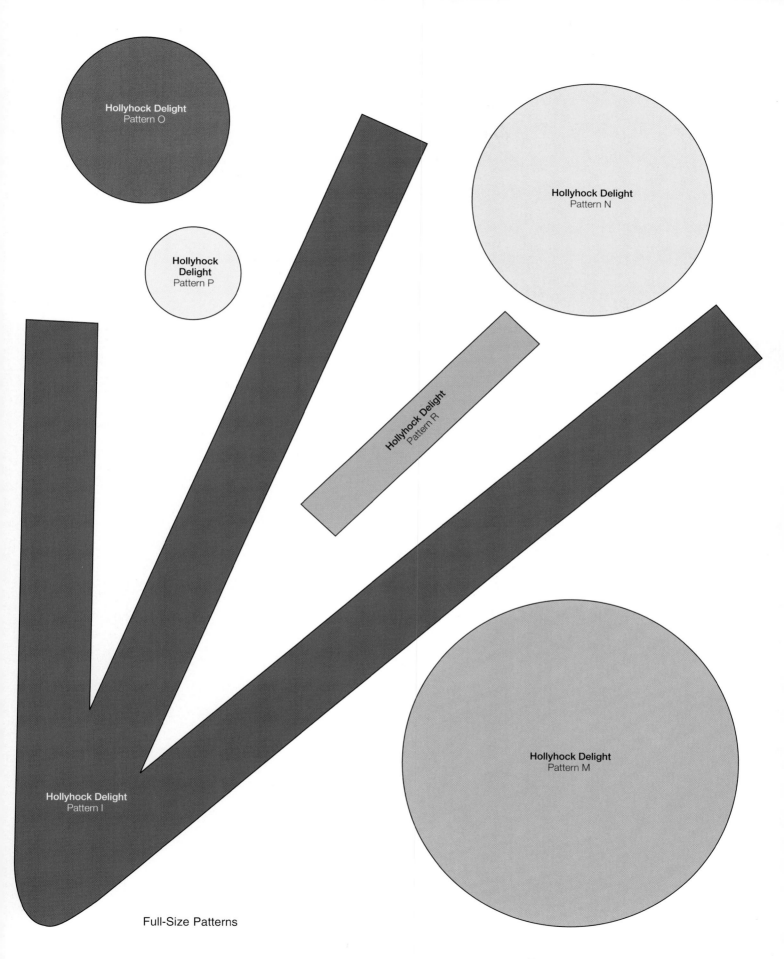

Hollyhock Delight
Pattern O

Hollyhock
Delight
Pattern P

Hollyhock Delight
Pattern N

Hollyhock Delight
Pattern R

Hollyhock Delight
Pattern I

Hollyhock Delight
Pattern M

Full-Size Patterns

Not only do the bright, fun colors make this a great gift for a young girl in your life, but appliquéd hearts, flowers, and plenty of hugs and kisses make it something she'll treasure forever.

Designer: Linda Lum Debono
Photographer: Perry Struse

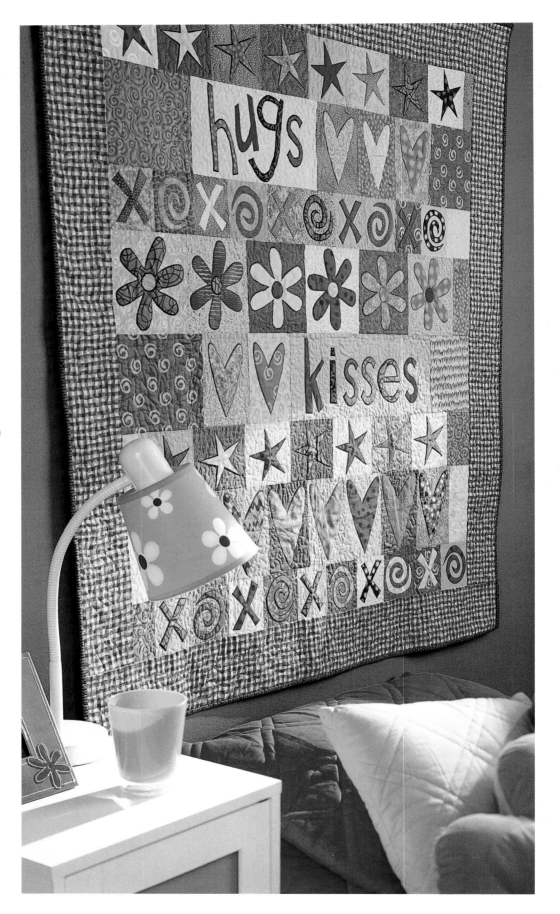

hugs and kisses

materials

2½ yards total of assorted bright prints for blocks and appliqués
1⅓ yards of pink plaid for border
½ yard of purple print for binding
2⅞ yards of backing fabric
51×54" of quilt batting
1 yard of lightweight fusible web

FINISHED QUILT: 45×48¼"

Quantities specified for 44/45"-wide, 100% cotton fabrics. All measurements include a ¼" seam allowance. Sew with right sides together unless otherwise stated.

cut the fabrics

To make the best use of your fabrics, cut the pieces in the order that follows. The patterns are on *pages 22–23*. To make templates of the patterns, follow the instructions in Appliqué Primer, which begins on *page 82*.

Cut the border strips the length of the fabric (parallel to the selvage).

To use fusible web for appliquéing, as was done in this project, complete the following steps.

1. Lay the fusible web, paper side up, over the patterns. Use a pencil to trace each pattern the number of times indicated, leaving ½" between tracings. Cut out each piece roughly ¼" outside the traced lines.

2. Following the manufacturer's instructions, press the fusible-web shapes onto the wrong sides of the designated fabrics; let cool. Cut out the fabric shapes on the drawn lines. Peel off the paper backings.

From assorted bright prints, cut:
- 1—16½×6½" rectangle for kisses appliqué foundation
- 1—12¼×6½" rectangle for hugs appliqué foundation
- 6—6¼×6½" rectangles for daisy appliqué foundations
- 15—5×4¾" rectangles for star appliqué foundations
- 8—4¾×6¾" rectangles for large heart appliqué foundations
- 5—4¾×6½" rectangles for small heart appliqué foundations
- 20—3¾×4¼" rectangles for X and spiral appliqué foundations
- 1—8×6½" rectangle for filler block
- 1—7½×6½" rectangle for filler block
- 1—6×6½" rectangle for filler block
- 1—5½×6½" rectangle for filler block
- 2—5×4¼" rectangles for filler blocks
- 1—3½×6¾" rectangle for filler block
- 1—3½×4¾" rectangle for filler block
- 1—3×6½" rectangle for filler block
- 1—3×4¾" rectangle for filler block
- 1—1½×4¾" rectangle for filler block
- 15 of Pattern A
- 5 of Pattern B
- 6 *each* of patterns C and D
- 10 *each* of patterns E and F
- 8 of Pattern G
- 1 *each* of letters e, g, h, i, k, and u
- 4 of the letter s

From pink plaid, cut:
- 2—4½×45½" border strips
- 2—4½×40¾" border strips

From purple print, cut:
- 5—2½×42" binding strips

appliqué the foundations

1. Referring to the Quilt Assembly Diagram on *page 20* for placement, arrange the appliqué shapes on the designated bright print foundations. Fuse in place.

2. Using color-coordinating thread, machine-stitch around the appliqué shapes with a short, narrow zigzag stitch.

assemble the quilt center

1. Referring to the Quilt Assembly Diagram, lay out the appliquéd foundations and the filler blocks in horizontal rows.

2. Sew together the pieces in each row. Press the seam allowances in each row in one direction, alternating the direction with each row.

3. Join the rows to make the quilt center. Press the seam allowances in one direction. The pieced quilt center should measure 37½×40¾", including the seam allowances.

add the border

1. Sew the pink plaid 4½×40¾" border strips to each side edge of the pieced quilt center. Press the seam allowances toward the border.

2. Then add the pink plaid 4½×45½" border strips to the top and bottom edges of the pieced quilt center to complete the quilt top. Press the seam allowances toward the border.

complete the quilt

1. Layer the quilt top, batting, and backing according to the directions in Quilting Basics, which begins on *page 94*.

2. Quilt as desired. Designer Linda Lum DeBono machine-stitched the quilt in a free-motion design.

3. Use the purple print 2½×42" strips to bind the quilt according to the instructions in Quilting Basics.

tic-tac-toe pillow

materials

Scraps of assorted bright prints for appliqués and appliqué foundations
18×22" piece (fat quarter) of fuchsia print for inner border and binding
⅔ yard of lime green print for outer border and pillow back
22" square of muslin for lining
22" square of quilt batting
16"-square pillow form

FINISHED PILLOW TOP: 16" square

cut the fabrics

To make the best use of your fabrics, cut the pieces in the order that follows. The patterns are on *pages 22–23*.

To prepare fusible web for appliquéing, see Cut the Fabrics, steps 1 and 2, on *page 19* and use the specified patterns and fabrics that follow.

From assorted bright prints, cut:
- 9—4½" squares for appliqué foundations
- 5 of Pattern E
- 4 of Pattern F

From fuchsia print, cut:
- 3—2½×22" binding strips
- 2—1×13½" inner border strips
- 2—1×12½" inner border strips

From lime green print, cut:
- 2—16½×20½" rectangles
- 2—2×16½" outer border strips
- 2—2×13½" outer border strips

appliqué the foundations

1. Arrange the appliqué shapes on the bright print 4½"-square foundations.

2. Fuse in place. Using color-coordinating thread, machine-stitch around the appliqué shapes with a short, narrow zigzag stitch.

assemble the pillow top

1. Referring to the photograph *opposite*, lay out the appliquéd squares in three horizontal rows. Join the pieces in each row, pressing the seam allowances toward the X squares. Then join the rows to make the pillow center. Press the seam allowances in one direction. The pillow center should measure 12½" square, including the seam allowances.

2. Sew the fuchsia print 1×12½" inner border strips to opposite edges of the pillow center. Then sew the fuchsia print 1×13½" inner border strips to the remaining edges of the pillow center. Press all seam allowances toward the inner border.

3. Sew the lime green print 2×13½" outer border strips to opposite edges of the pillow center. Then sew the lime green print 2×16½" outer border strips to the remaining edges of the pillow center to complete the pillow top. Press the seam allowances toward the outer border.

complete the pillow

1. Layer the pillow top, batting, and muslin 22"-square lining according to the directions in Quilting Basics, which begins on *page 94*.

2. Quilt as desired. Trim batting and lining even with the pillow top edges.

3. Turn one short edge of each lime green print 16½×20½" rectangle under ¼". Topstitch the folded edges in place.

4. With right sides up, layer one hemmed lime green print rectangle over the other so

Quilt Assembly Diagram

that the stitched edges overlap about 3" to make a pillow back that measures 16½" square. Baste the edges where the pieces overlap.

5. With wrong sides together, layer the pillow top and pillow back; baste in place. Use the fuchsia print 2½×22" strips to bind the pillow according to the instructions in Quilting Basics.

6. Insert the pillow form through the opening in the pillow back.

daisy pillow

materials

Scraps of assorted bright prints for appliqués and appliqué foundations
9×22" piece (fat eighth) of apricot print for inner border
⅔ yard of orange print for outer border and pillow back
9×22" piece (fat eighth) of lime green print for binding
22" square of muslin for lining
22" square of quilt batting
16"-square pillow form

FINISHED PILLOW TOP: 16" square

cut the fabrics

To make the best use of your fabrics, cut the pieces in the order that follows. The patterns are on *pages 22–23*.

To prepare fusible web for appliquéing, see Cut the Fabrics, steps 1 and 2, on *page 19* and use the specified patterns and fabrics that follow.

From assorted bright prints, cut:
● 4—6½" squares for appliqué foundations
● 4 of Pattern C
● 28 of Pattern D
From apricot print, cut:
● 2—1×13½" inner border strips
● 2—1×12½" inner border strips
From orange print, cut:
● 2—16½×20½" rectangles
● 2—2×16½" outer border strips
● 2—2×13½" outer border strips

From lime green print:
● 3—2½×22" binding strips

assemble the pillow top

Referring to the directions on page 20 and the photograph *above*, appliqué each bright print 6½" square foundation with a daisy flower and center. Appliqué the orange print outer border strips with daisy centers. Sew together the four appliquéd foundations; add the borders to make the pillow top.

complete the pillow

1. Layer the pillow top, batting, and muslin 22"-square lining according to the directions in Quilting Basics, which begins on *page 94*.

2. Quilt as desired. Trim batting and lining even with the pillow top edges.

3. Turn one short edge of each orange print 16½×20½" rectangle under ¼". Topstitch the folded edges in place.

4. With right sides up, layer one hemmed orange print rectangle over the other so that the stitched edges overlay about 3" to make a pillow back that measures 16½" square. Baste the edges where the pieces overlap.

5. With wrong sides together, layer the pillow top and pillow back; baste in place. Use the lime green print 2½×22" strips to bind the pillow according to the instructions in Quilting Basics.

6. Insert the pillow form through the opening in the pillow back.

Hugs and Kisses
Pattern F

Hugs and Kisses
Pattern D

Hugs and Kisses
Pattern C

Hugs and Kisses
Pattern G

Hugs and Kisses
Pattern B

Hugs and Kisses
Pattern A

Full-Size Patterns

Hugs and Kisses
Pattern E

peony
wall hanging

Practice your machine-appliqué skills on the curving vines and shapely peonies of this cheery quilt. Its sunny yellow background and pretty scalloped border make it a nice addition to any room.

Photographer: Craig Anderson

materials

- 1 yard total of assorted blue prints for appliqués and inner border corner squares
- 18×22" (fat quarter) of pink print for appliqués
- 9×22" (fat eighth) of dark pink print for appliqués
- 18×22" (fat quarter) of orange tone-on-tone print for appliqués
- 1/8 yard total of assorted yellow prints for appliqués
- 1/4 yard each of two light green prints for appliqué foundations and sashing
- 1/4 yard of bright yellow print for sashing
- 1/4 yard of orange print for inner border
- 5/8 yard of light blue print for middle border
- 1½ yards of large floral for outer border
- 5/8 yard of lime green print for binding
- 3 yards of backing fabric
- 57×53" of quilt batting
- 1 yard of lightweight fusible web

FINISHED QUILT: 51×46½"

cut the fabrics

To make the best use of your fabrics, cut the pieces in the order that follows. The patterns are on *page 27*. To make templates of these patterns, follow the instructions in Appliqué Primer, which begins on *page 82*.

To use fusible web for appliquéing, as was done in this project, complete the following steps.

1. Lay the fusible web, paper side up, over the patterns. Use a pencil to trace each pattern the number of times indicated, leaving ½" between tracings. Cut out each piece roughly ¼" outside the traced lines.

2. Following the manufacturer's instructions, press the fusible-web shapes onto the wrong sides of the designated fabrics; let cool. Cut out the fabric shades on the drawn lines. Peel off the paper backings.

From assorted blue prints, cut:
- 1—14" square, cutting it into enough ¾"-wide bias strips to make a 200"-long vine appliqué
- 1—10" square, cutting it into enough ¾"-wide bias strips to make six ¾×7" strips for large flower stems (For specific instructions on cutting bias strips, see Appliqué Primer.)
- 4—2" squares
- 20 of Pattern A
- 35 of Pattern B
- 16 of Pattern F

From pink print, cut:
- 3 of Pattern E

From dark pink print, cut:
- 6 of Pattern F

From orange tone-on-tone print, cut:
- 3 of Pattern C

From assorted yellow prints, cut:
- 16 of Pattern E

From each light green print, cut:
- 3—8½×10½" rectangles for appliqué foundations
- 2—1" squares

From bright yellow print, cut:
- 2—1×25½" sashing strips
- 4—1×21" sashing strips
- 3—1×8½" sashing strips

From orange print, cut:
- 2—2×26½" inner border strips
- 2—2×22" inner border strips

From light blue print, cut:
- 2—4½×37½" middle border strips
- 2—4½×25" middle border strips

From large floral, cut:
- 2—7½×51½" outer border strips
- 2—7½×33" outer border strips

From lime green print, cut:
- 1—18×24" rectangle, cutting it into enough 2½"-wide bias strips to total 210" in length

appliqué the blocks

1. Prepare the blue print stem and vine appliqué pieces by basting under a 3/16" seam allowance. Set aside the vine appliqué piece.

2. Referring to the Appliqué Placement Diagram on *page 26* for placement, arrange a prepared stem on a light green 8½×10½" rectangle; baste. Machine-blanket-stitch the stem in place. Arrange the remaining appliqué pieces on the foundation; fuse. Machine-blanket-stitch the remaining appliqué pieces in place to complete an appliquéd block.

3. Repeat Step 2 to make a total of six appliquéd blocks.

assemble the quilt center

1. Referring to the photograph *opposite*, lay out the six appliquéd blocks and three bright yellow print 1×8½" sashing strips in vertical rows. Join the rows with two bright yellow print 1×21" sashing strips between the rows to make a pieced block unit. Press all seam allowances toward the sashing strips.

2. Add the bright yellow print 1×25½" sashing strips to the top and bottom edges of the pieced block unit. Join a light green print 1" square to each end of the remaining bright yellow print 1×21" sashing strips to make two sashing units. Add the sashing units to the side edges of the pieced block unit to complete the quilt center. The pieced quilt center should measure 26½×22", including the seam allowances.

add the borders

1. Sew the orange print 2×26½" inner border strips to the top and bottom edges of the quilt center. Join a blue print 2" square to each end of the orange print 2×22" inner border strips to make inner border units. Add the inner border units to the side edges of the quilt center.

2. Sew the light blue print 4½×25" middle border strips to the side edges of the quilt center. Add the light blue print 4½×37½" middle border strips to the top and bottom edges of the quilt center. Press all seam allowances toward the middle border.

3. Sew the large floral 7½×33" outer border strips to the side edges of the quilt center. Then add the large floral 7½×51½" outer border strips to the top and bottom edges of the quilt center to complete the quilt top. Press all seam allowances toward the middle border.

appliqué the borders

1. Referring to the Appliqué Placement Diagram at *right* for placement, lay the prepared vine appliqué on the light blue middle border; baste. Machine-blanket-stitch in place.

2. Arrange the remaining appliqué pieces along the vine; fuse. Machine-blanket-stitch in place.

complete the quilt

Mark the scallops on the large floral outer border according to the following instructions. Do not cut the scallops until after quilting is completed.

1. Draw the desired scallop on a strip of paper as long as a border. Place three dots approximately 17" apart on the top edge of the paper to mark the top of each scallop. Draw a line between these dots. Make another set of dots 3½" directly below the first marks. The depth between the first and second marks is the depth of the scallops.

2. Using a compass, jar lid, plate, or other rounded edge as a guide, join the second set of marks with a gentle curve that just touches the line drawn between the first set of marks.

3. Once you've created a scallop you like, draw it along the complete length of the paper strip to make a border template. Repeat to make a side border template.

4. Position the paper templates on the quilt top outer border and check the corners. You'll need to blend the curves of the scallops to round the corners. Once you've blended the edges of one corner, make a paper template of it and trace three more identical paper templates for the remaining corners. Use your paper templates to mark the pattern on your quilt top outer border.

5. Hand- or machine-quilt as desired. Trim the outer border according to the marked scallops, leaving ¼" beyond the drawn line.

6. Use the lime green print 2½"-wide bias strips to bind the quilt according to the instructions in Quilting Basics, which begins on *page 94*.

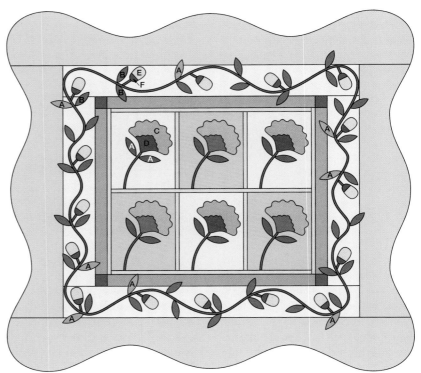

Appliqué Placement Diagram

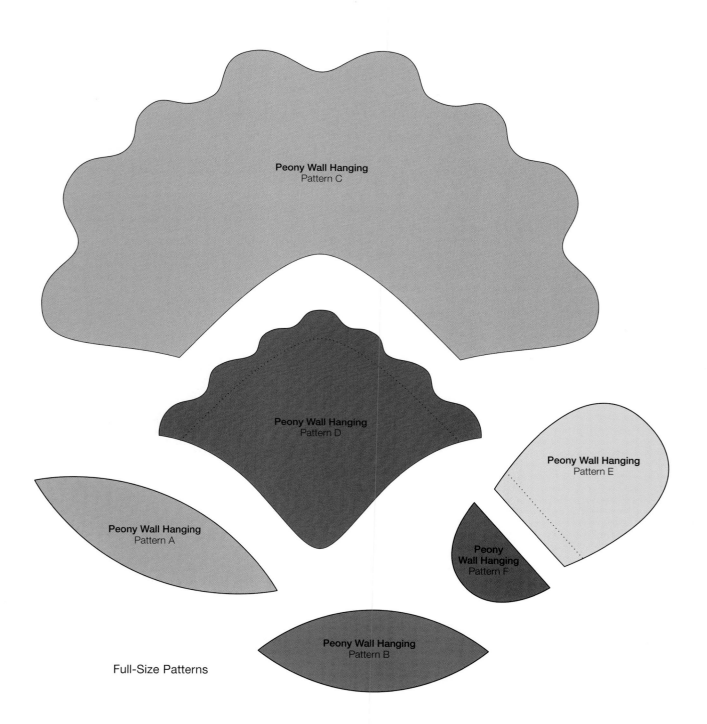

Peony Wall Hanging
Pattern C

Peony Wall Hanging
Pattern D

Peony Wall Hanging
Pattern E

Peony Wall Hanging
Pattern A

**Peony
Wall Hanging**
Pattern F

Peony Wall Hanging
Pattern B

Full-Size Patterns

playball!

Indulge your favorite sports fanatic with this oversize flannel throw. Decked out with sports gear for any season, it'll be a favorite for curling up with while watching the big game.

Designer: Lynne Hagmeier
Photographer: Perry Struse

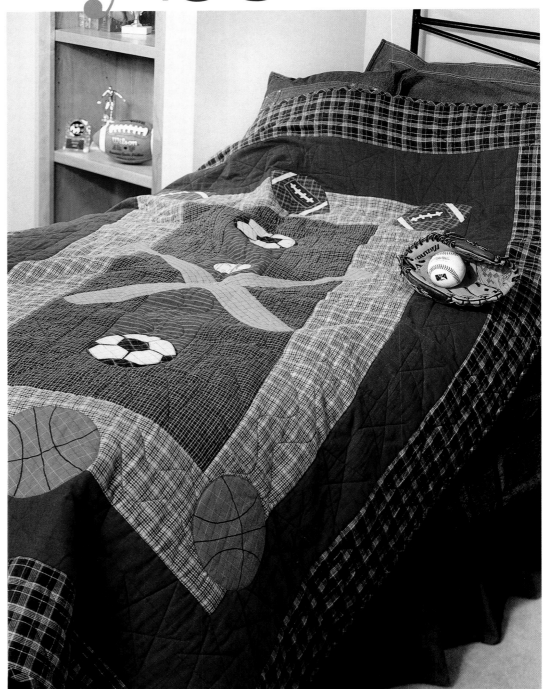

materials

¼ yard of red plaid flannel No. 1 for center rectangle

⅝ yard of blue plaid flannel No. 1 for inner border

1½ yards of tan-and-blue plaid flannel for second border

1¾ yards of red plaid flannel No. 2 for third border

3 yards of blue plaid flannel No. 2 for outer border and binding

2—9×22" pieces (fat eighths) of dark brown plaids for football appliqués

9×22" piece (fat eighth) of off-white plaid for football and soccer ball appliqués

9×22" piece (fat eighth) of black plaid for football and soccer ball appliqués

¼ yard of brown plaid for baseball bat appliqués

Scrap of tan plaid for baseball appliqué

9×22" piece (fat eighth) of orange plaid for basketball appliqués

5 yards of backing fabric

60×90" of quilt batting

1½ yards of lightweight fusible web

FINISHED QUILT: 54×84"

Quantities specified for 44/45"-wide, 100% cotton fabrics. All measurements include a ¼" seam allowance. Sew with right sides together unless otherwise stated.

cut the fabrics

To make the best use of your fabrics, cut the pieces in the order that follows. Cut the second, third, and outer border strips the length of the fabric (parallel to the selvage).

From red plaid flannel No. 1, cut:
- 1—6½×36½" rectangle

From blue plaid flannel No. 1, cut:
- 2—6½×36½" inner border strips
- 2—6½×18½" inner border strips

From tan-and-blue plaid flannel, cut:
- 2—6½×48½" second border strips
- 2—6½×30½" second border strips

From red plaid flannel No. 2, cut:
- 2—6½×60½" third border strips
- 2—6½×42½" third border strips

From blue plaid flannel No. 2, cut:
- 2—6½×72½" outer border strips
- 2—6½×54½" outer border strips
- 1—30" square, cutting it in enough 2¾"-wide bias strips to total 285" in length for binding (For specific instructions on cutting bias strips, see page 86 in the Appliqué Primer.)

assemble the quilt top

1. Referring to the Quilt Assembly Diagram on *page 30* for placement, sew the blue plaid flannel No. 1 6½×36½" inner border strips to the side edges of the red plaid flannel 6½×36½" rectangle. Then join the blue plaid flannel No. 1 6½×18½" border strips to the top and bottom edges of the red plaid rectangle. Press all seam allowances toward the border.

2. In the same manner, add the tan-and-blue plaid flannel second border strips, the red plaid flannel No. 2 third border strips, and the blue plaid flannel No. 2 outer border strips to make the quilt top. The pieced quilt top should measure 54½×84½", including the seam allowances.

complete the quilt

1. Layer the quilt top, batting, and backing according to the instructions in Quilting Basics, which begins on *page 94*.

2. Quilt as desired. Quilter Nancy Arnoldy machine-quilted wavy lines freehand in the center red plaid flannel rectangle, in the second border, and in the outer border. She machine-quilted stars in the inner and third borders.

3. Use the blue plaid flannel 2¾"-wide bias strips to bind the quilt according to the instructions in Quilting Basics.

prepare the sports appliqués

The patterns are on *pages 31–33*. To make templates of the patterns, follow the instructions in Appliqué Primer, which begins on *page 82*.

To use fusible web for appliquéing, as was done in this project, complete the following steps.

1. Lay the fusible web, paper side up, over the patterns. Use a pencil to trace each pattern the number of times indicated, leaving ½" between tracings. Cut out each piece roughly ¼" outside the traced lines.

2. Following the manufacturer's instructions, press the fusible-web shapes onto the wrong sides of the designated fabrics; let cool. Cut out the fabric shapes on the drawn lines. Peel off the paper backings.

From *one* dark brown plaid, cut:
● 3 of Pattern A
From a second dark brown plaid, cut:
● 3 of Pattern B
From off-white plaid, cut:
● 3 of Pattern C

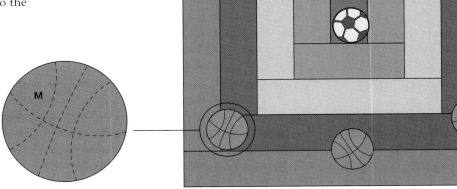

Quilt Assembly Diagram

● 6 of Pattern D
● 2 *each* of patterns F, G, H, I, J
From black plaid, cut:
● 2 of Pattern E
From brown plaid, cut:
● 2 of Pattern K
From tan plaid, cut:
● 1 of Pattern L
From orange plaid, cut:
● 3 of Pattern M

"appliquilt" the quilt

1. Referring to the Quilt Assembly Diagram, *above*, arrange the appliqué shapes on the

quilt, layering the trims on the footballs and soccer balls as shown; fuse in place.

2. Using matching thread, machine-appliqué the shapes in place. Lynne blanket-stitched the outside edges of the appliqués and the footballs' dark brown plaid trim pieces. She used a straight stitch on the footballs' off-white plaid and trim pieces and the soccer balls' trim pieces.

3. Create the basketballs' seams using a narrow zigzag stitch; use a featherstitch to make the baseball's seams.

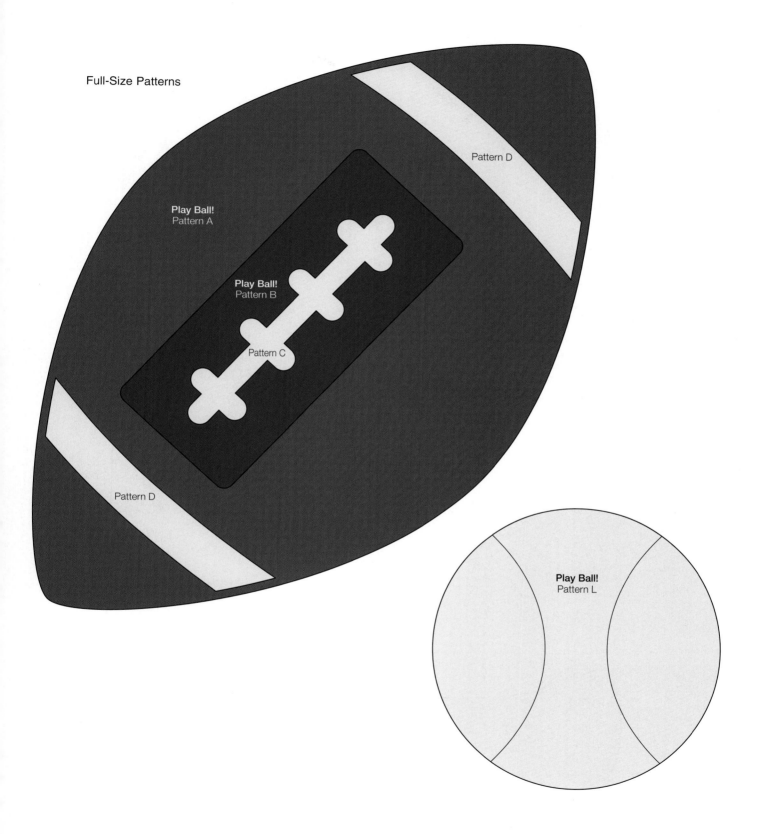

Full-Size Patterns

Play Ball!
Pattern A

Play Ball!
Pattern B

Pattern C

Pattern D

Pattern D

Play Ball!
Pattern L

Full-Size Patterns

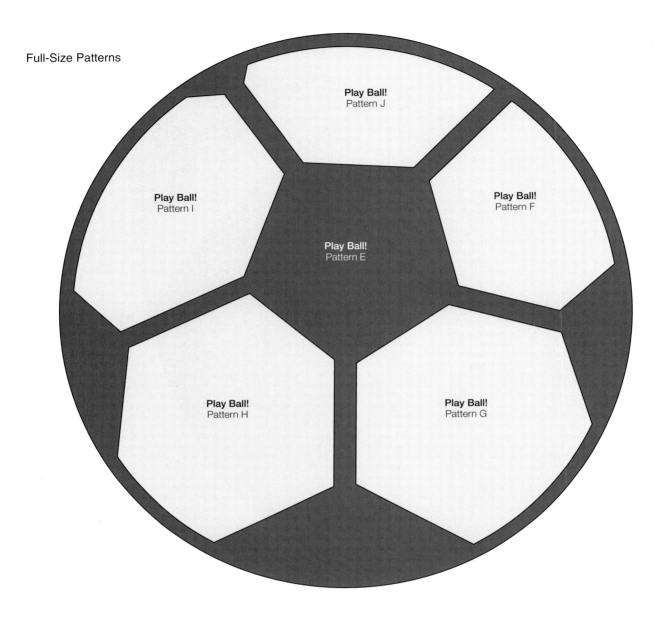

Play Ball!
Pattern J

Play Ball!
Pattern I

Play Ball!
Pattern F

Play Ball!
Pattern E

Play Ball!
Pattern H

Play Ball!
Pattern G

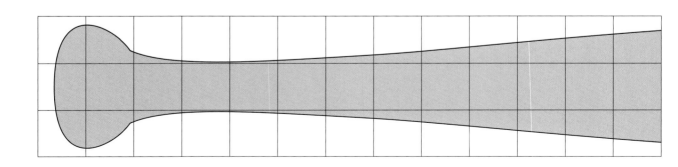

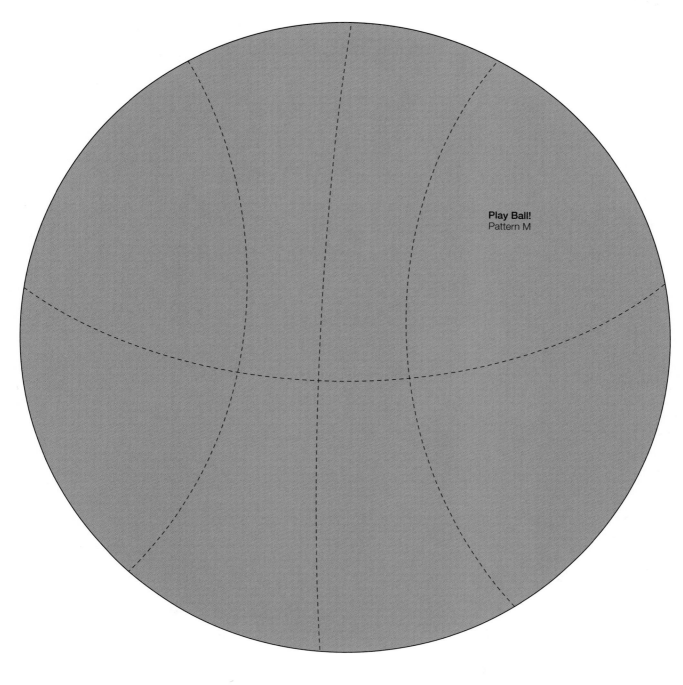

Play Ball!
Pattern M

Play Ball!
Pattern K

1 Square = 1 Inch
Enlarge @ 200%

spring fling

Simple basket and flower shapes are fused to an array of pink and brown fabrics on this machine-appliquéd wall hanging.

Designers: Avis Shirer and
   Tammy Johnson
Photographer: Perry Struse

materials

- 2—9×22" pieces (fat eighths) of assorted dusty pink prints for basket appliqué foundations
- 3—9×22" pieces (fat eighths) of assorted brown prints for basket and star appliqués
- 4—1/8-yard pieces of assorted gold stripes for appliqués and appliqué foundations
- 4—9×22" pieces (fat eighths) of assorted tan prints for appliqué foundations
- 8—9×22" pieces (fat eighths) of assorted pink prints and burgundy prints for triangle-squares and flower appliqués
- 1/2 yard of burgundy print No. 1 for flower appliqués and binding
- 9×22" piece (fat eighth) of solid green for stem appliqués
- 9×22" piece (fat eighth) of green print for leaf appliqués
- 1/4 yard of pink-and-brown plaid for inner border
- 1/2 yard of burgundy print No. 2 for outer border
- 1 1/8 yards of backing fabric
- 38×42" of quilt batting
- 2 yards of lightweight fusible web

FINISHED QUILT TOP: 35½×31½"

Quantities specified for 44/45"-wide, 100% cotton fabrics. All measurements include a ¼" seam allowance. Sew with right sides together unless otherwise stated.

cut the fabrics

To make the best use of your fabrics, cut the pieces in the order that follows. The border strip measurements are mathematically correct. You may wish to cut your strips longer than specified to allow for possible sewing differences.

The patterns are on *pages 37–39*. To use fusible web for appliquéing, as was done in this project, complete the following steps.

1. Lay the fusible web, paper side up, over the patterns. Use a pencil to trace each pattern the number of times indicated, leaving ½" between tracings. Cut out each piece roughly ¼" outside the traced lines.

2. Following the manufacturer's instructions, press the fusible-web shapes onto the wrong sides of the designated fabrics; let cool. Cut out the fabric shapes on the drawn lines. Peel off the paper backings.

From assorted dusty pink prints, cut:
- 2—6½×16½" rectangles for basket appliqué foundations

From assorted brown prints, cut:
- 1 *each* of patterns A and A reversed
- 6 of Pattern B

From assorted gold stripes, cut:
- 6—4½" squares for star appliqué foundations
- 4 of Pattern H

From assorted tan prints, cut:
- 4—8½" squares for flower appliqué foundations

From *each* of the 8 assorted pink and burgundy prints, cut:
- 1—4⅞" square, cutting it in half diagonally to make 2 triangles

From remaining assorted pink and burgundy print scraps, cut:
- 4 each of patterns D, E, F, and G

From burgundy print No. 1, cut:
- 4—2½×42" binding strips
- 4 of Pattern C

From solid green, cut:
- 2 *each* of patterns I and I reversed

From green print, cut:
- 2 *each* of patterns J and J reversed

From pink-and-brown plaid, cut:
- 2—1¼×28½" inner border strips
- 2—1¼×26" inner border strips

From burgundy print No. 2, cut:
- 2—3½×32" outer border strips
- 2—3½×30" outer border strips

appliqué the blocks

1. Referring to Diagram 1, *right*, for placement, arrange each brown print A basket on a dusty pink print 6½×16½" appliqué foundation; fuse in place.

2. Using thread in a color that matches the appliqué fabric, machine-blanket-stitch the appliqués in place.

3. Repeat steps 1 and 2 to appliqué each assorted brown print star to an assorted gold stripe 4½" square.

4. Repeat steps 1 and 2 to fuse the flower, leaf, and stem shapes to the assorted tan print 8½" square appliqué foundations. Stitch the pieces in place, working from the bottom layer to the top.

assemble the triangle-squares

1. Join one pink print and one burgundy print triangle to make a triangle-square (see Diagram 2). Press the seam allowance toward the burgundy print triangle. The pieced triangle-square should measure 4½" square, including the seam allowances.

Diagram 2

2. Repeat to make a total of eight triangle-squares.

assemble the quilt center

1. Referring to Diagram 1, *above right*, for placement, lay out the appliquéd blocks and triangle-squares in three horizontal rows. Sew together the pieces in each row. Press the seam allowances in one direction, alternating the direction with each row.

Diagram 1

2. Join the rows to make the quilt center. Press the seam allowances in one direction. The pieced quilt center should measure 24½×28½", including the seam allowances.

add the borders

1. Sew the pink-and-brown plaid 1¼×28½" inner border strips to the top and bottom edges of the pieced quilt center. Then add the pink-and-brown plaid 1¼×26" inner border strips to the side edges of the pieced quilt center. Press the seam allowances toward the pink-and-brown plaid border.

2. Sew the burgundy print 3½×30" outer border strips to the top and bottom edges of the pieced quilt center. Then add the burgundy print 3½×32" outer border strips to the side edges of the pieced quilt center to complete the quilt top. Press the seam allowances toward the burgundy print border.

complete the quilt

1. Layer the quilt top, batting, and backing according to the instructions in Quilting Basics, which begins on *page 94*. Quilt as desired.

2. Use the burgundy print 2½×42" strips to bind the quilt according to the instructions in Quilting Basics.

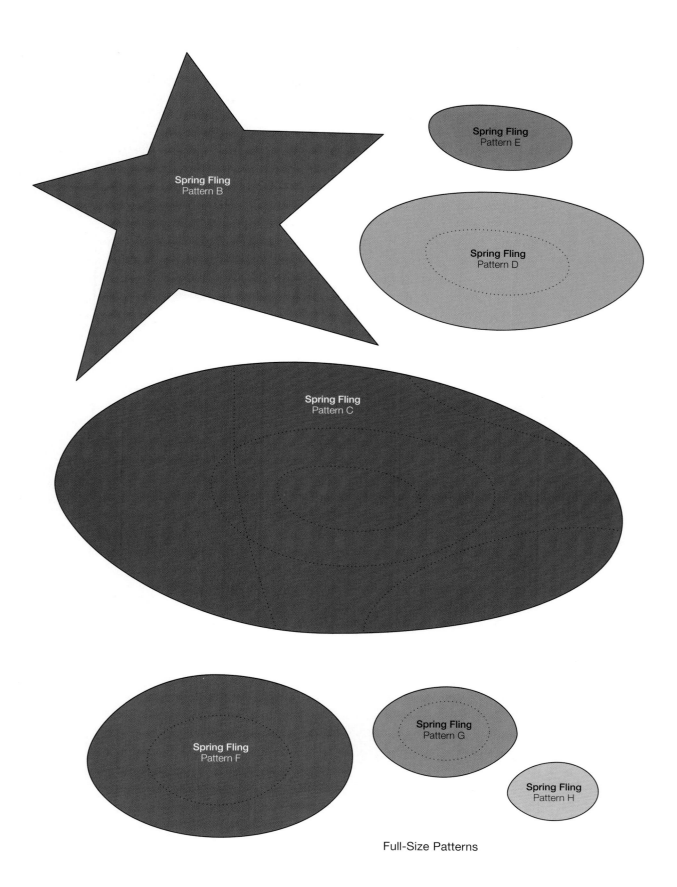

Spring Fling
Pattern B

Spring Fling
Pattern E

Spring Fling
Pattern D

Spring Fling
Pattern C

Spring Fling
Pattern F

Spring Fling
Pattern G

Spring Fling
Pattern H

Full-Size Patterns

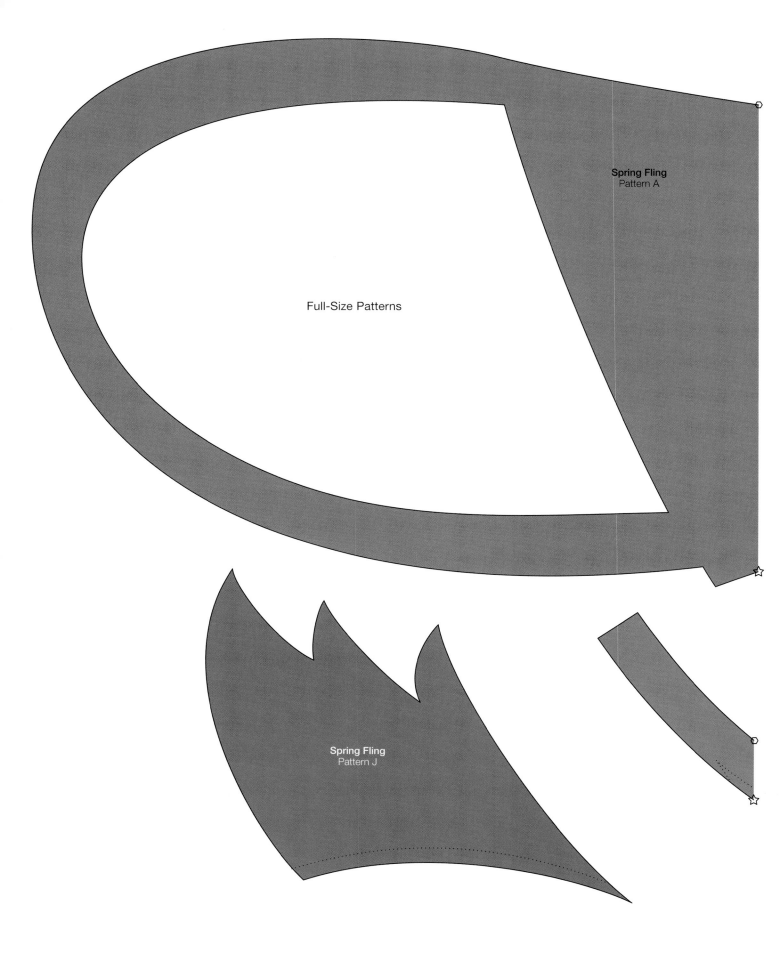

Full-Size Patterns

Spring Fling
Pattern A

Spring Fling
Pattern J

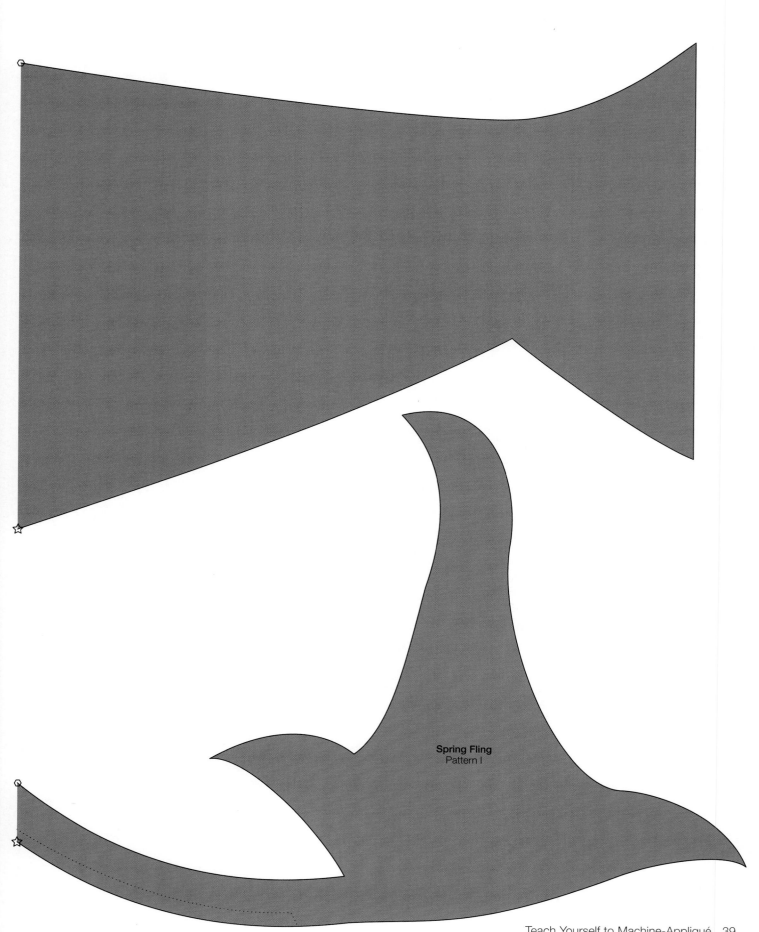

Spring Fling
Pattern I

table linens

Brighten
up a plain
purchased
tablecloth
with a
harvest of
cherry red
tomato
appliqués
and a
winding
vine
border.

Designer:
Diane Hansen

Photographer:
Scott Little

materials

Scraps of solid red for tomato appliqués
⅓ yard of green print for vine appliqué
Green embroidery floss
70"-diameter white tablecloth
4 dinner napkins
Lightweight fusible web
Machine embroidery thread in matching
   colors

cut the fabrics

To make the best use of your fabrics, cut the pieces in the order that follows.

   To use fusible web for appliquéing, as was done in this project, complete the following steps.

1. Lay the fusible web, paper side up, over the pattern, *far right.* Use a pencil to trace the pattern 34 times, leaving ½" between tracings. Cut out each piece roughly ¼" outside the traced lines.

2. Following the manufacturer's instructions, press the fusible-web shapes onto the wrong sides of the solid red fabric; let cool. Cut out the fabric shapes on the drawn lines. Peel off the paper backings.

From green print, cut:
● 2—12" squares, cutting them into enough 1½"-wide bias strips to total 240" in length (For specific instructions on cutting bias strips, see Appliqué Primer, which begins on *page 82.*)

3. Fold each green print 1½"-wide bias strip in half lengthwise with the wrong side inside and press.

4. Sew the long edges of each folded strip together. Trim each seam allowance to ⅛". Roll each seam allowance to the center of its strip; press the seam allowance to one side so that neither the seam nor the seam allowance is visible along the edges.

5. Position the prepared vine along the edge of the tablecloth, between 3" and 7" from the outer edge of the tablecloth. Baste in place. Machine-appliqué the vine in place.

6. Position the solid red circles along either side of the stitched vine; fuse in place. Fuse each remaining solid red circle to a napkin corner.

7. Machine-satin-stitch around the edges of all the solid red circles.

8. Using two strands of green embroidery floss and lazy daisy stitches, add four stitches to the center of each solid red circle to make a cherry tomato.

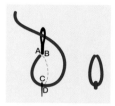

Lazy Daisy Stitch

   To make a lazy daisy stitch (see diagram *above*), pull the needle up at A and form a loop of thread on the fabric surface. Holding the loop in place, insert the needle back into the fabric at B, about 1/16" away from A. Bring the needle tip out at C and cross it over the trailing thread, keeping the thread as flat as possible. Gently pull the needle and trailing thread until the loop lies flat against the fabric. Push the needle through to the back at D to secure the loop in place.

Table Linens
Circle Pattern

whig rose

Red and green flowers bloom in a dramatic center medallion on this wall hanging. Inspired by an heirloom quilt, this modern version employs machine appliqué.

Designer: Betty Alderman   Photographer: Scott Little

materials

1½ yards of mottled pale yellow for center and outer border appliqué foundations

⅜ yard of pale green check for inner border and leaf appliqués

⅝ yard of red polka dot for middle border, flower appliqués, and binding

¼ yard of solid red for flower appliqués

¼ yard of solid green for leaf and stem appliqués

½ yard of solid light green for vine and stem appliqués

8" square of red check for large circle appliqué

¼ yard of yellow check for outer border corner appliqué foundations and flower center appliqués

Scrap of solid yellow for small circle appliqué

1⅛ yards of backing fabric

40" square of quilt batting

2 yards of lightweight fusible web

FINISHED QUILT TOP: 34½" square

Quantities specified for 44/45"-wide, 100% cotton fabrics. All measurements include a ¼" seam allowance. Sew with right sides together unless otherwise stated.

cut the fabrics

To make the best use of your fabrics, cut the pieces in the order that follows. The patterns are on *pages 45–47*.

To use fusible web for appliquéing, as was done in this project, complete the following steps.

1. Lay the fusible web, paper side up, over the patterns. Use a pencil to trace each pattern the number of times indicated, leaving ½" between tracings. Cut out each piece roughly ¼" outside the traced lines.

2. Following the manufacturer's instructions, press the fusible-web shapes onto the wrong sides of the designated fabrics; let cool. Cut out the fabric shapes on the drawn lines. Peel off the paper backings.

From mottled pale yellow, cut:
- 4—6½×23" outer border strips
- 1—20" square

From pale green check, cut:
- 2—1½×22" inner border strips
- 2—1½×20" inner border strips
- 4 of Pattern E
- 16 of Pattern H
- 22 of Pattern M

From red polka dot, cut:
- 4—2½×42" binding strips
- 2—1×23" middle border strips
- 2—1×22" middle border strips
- 1 *each* of patterns C and K
- 8 of Pattern F

From solid red, cut:
- 4 of Pattern I
- 11 of Pattern K

From solid green, cut:
- 4 of Pattern D
- 8 of Pattern L

From solid light green, cut:
- 4 *each* of patterns, G and L
- 8 of Pattern O
- 12 of Pattern N

From red check, cut:
- 1 of Pattern A

From yellow check, cut:
- 4—6½" squares
- 16 of Pattern J

From solid yellow, cut:
- 1 of Pattern B

appliqué the quilt center

1. Referring to the Whig Rose Assembly Diagram on *page 44* for placement, lay out the necessary appliqué shapes on the mottled pale yellow 20" square appliqué foundation. Fuse the shapes in place.

2. Using threads in colors that match the appliqué fabrics and a satin or blanket stitch, machine-appliqué the pieces to the foundation to make the quilt center. If your fabric puckers as you stitch, you may need to place a stabilizer under the appliqué foundation. If so, remove it after you've completed the appliqué.

3. In the same manner, appliqué the four mottled pale yellow 6½×23" outer border strips and the yellow check 6½" square outer border corners, referring to the Whig Rose Assembly Diagram for placement.

add the borders

1. Sew the pale green check 1½×20" inner border strips to the top and bottom edges of the appliquéd quilt center. Then add the pale green check 1½×22" strips to the side edges of the quilt center. Press all seam allowances toward the pale green inner border.

2. Sew the red polka-dot 1×22" middle border strips to the top and bottom edges of the appliquéd quilt center. Then add the red polka-dot 1×23" strips to the side edges of the quilt center. Press all seam allowances toward the red polka-dot middle border.

3. Sew the appliquéd 6½×23" outer border strips to opposite edges of the appliquéd quilt center, carefully noting the placement of the appliqués. Press the seam allowances toward the red polka-dot middle border.

4. Add an appliquéd 6½" square outer border corner to each end of the remaining appliquéd outer border strips to make two outer border units. Press the seam allowances toward the corner squares. Add an outer border unit to the remaining edges of the quilt center to complete the quilt top.

complete the quilt

1. Layer the quilt top, batting, and backing according to the instructions in Quilting Basics, which begins on *page 94*.

2. Quilt as desired. Designer Betty Alderman hand-quilted her project, stitching in the ditch around all the appliqué designs. She echo-quilted the center motif and the border vines, spacing her rows about ½" apart.

3. Use the red polka-dot 2½×42" strips to bind the quilt according to the instructions in Quilting Basics.

Whig Rose Assembly Diagram

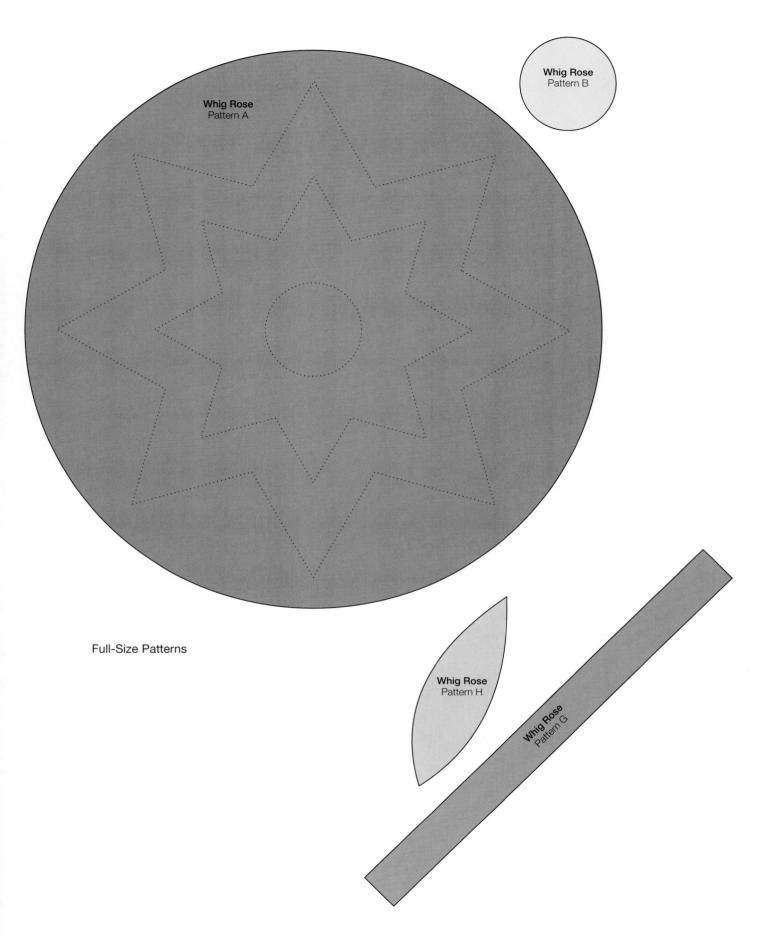

Whig Rose
Pattern A

Whig Rose
Pattern B

Whig Rose
Pattern H

Whig Rose
Pattern G

Full-Size Patterns

Whig Rose
Pattern C

Full-Size Patterns

Whig Rose
Pattern J

Whig Rose
Pattern K

Whig Rose
Pattern I

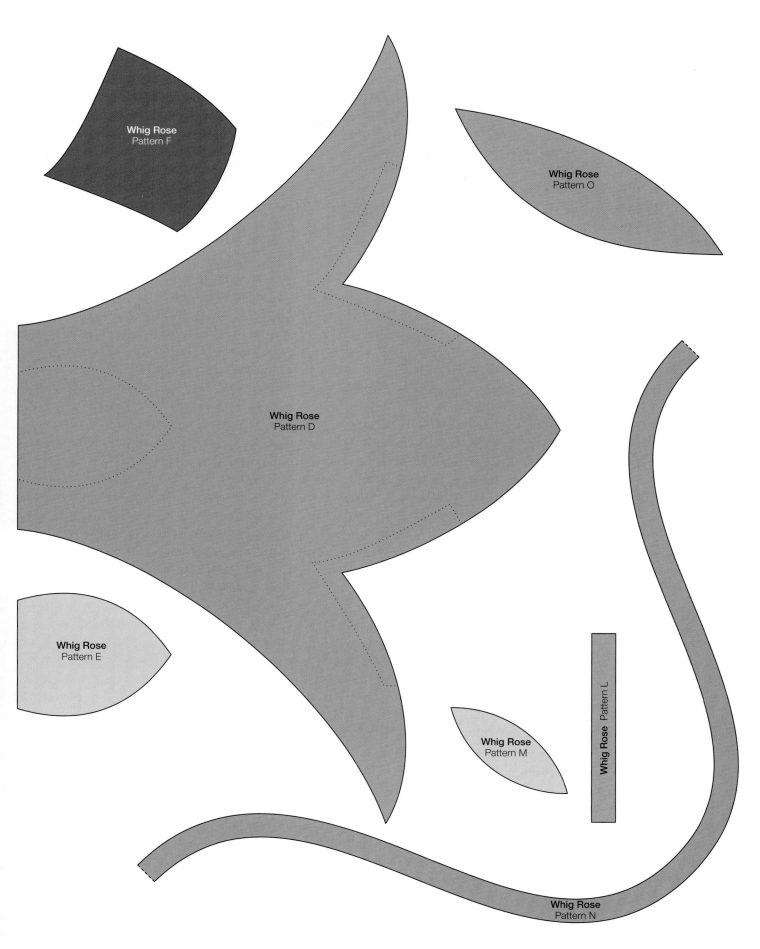

Whig Rose
Pattern F

Whig Rose
Pattern O

Whig Rose
Pattern D

Whig Rose
Pattern E

Whig Rose
Pattern M

Whig Rose Pattern L

Whig Rose
Pattern N

Proudly display your love for America with this simple rotary-cut banner embellished with an appliquéd greeting and trio of stars. Patterns make cutting the large gold stars easy.

Designer: Diane Hansen
Photographer: Scott Little

true-blue welcome

materials

⅛ yard total of assorted cream prints for blocks and letter appliqués

⅝ yard total of assorted dark red prints for blocks and appliqué foundations

Scrap of navy-and-white star print for block

¼ yard total of assorted gold prints for blocks and star appliqués

Scraps of five assorted navy prints for blocks and appliqué foundation

Scrap of tan print No. 1 for blocks

9×22" piece (fat eighth) of tan print No. 2 for appliqué foundation

¼ yard of navy plaid for border

¼ yard of dark navy print for binding

⅞ yard of backing fabric

28×41" of quilt batting

⅓ yard of lightweight fusible web

FINISHED QUILT: 22×35"

Quantities specified for 44/45"-wide, 100% cotton fabrics. All measurements include a ¼" seam allowance. Sew with right sides together unless otherwise stated.

cut the fabrics

To make the best use of your fabrics, cut the pieces in the order that follows.

The patterns are on *pages 51-52*. To use fusible web for appliquéing, as was done in this project, complete the following steps.

1. Lay the fusible web, paper side up, over the patterns. Use a pencil to trace each pattern the number of times indicated, leaving ½" between tracings. Cut out each piece roughly ¼" outside the traced lines. To reduce bulk in the Pattern C pieces, cut ¼" inside the traced lines and discard the centers.

2. Following the manufacturer's instructions, press the fusible-web shapes onto the wrong sides of the designated fabrics; let cool. Cut out the fabric shapes on the drawn lines. Peel off the paper backings.

From assorted cream prints, cut:
● 1—6½×1½" rectangle
● 2—3½×1½" rectangles
● 1 *each* of the letters C, L, M, O, and W
● 2 of the letter E

From assorted dark red prints, cut:
● 1—1½×42" strip
● 4—4⅞" squares, cutting each in half diagonally for a total of 8 triangles
● 2—6½×4½" rectangles
● 2—6½×1½" rectangles
● 1—3½×1½" rectangle
● 8—2½" squares
● 4 of Pattern A

From navy-and-white star print, cut:
● 1—3½" square

From assorted gold prints, cut:
● 4 *each* of patterns B and B reversed
● 3 of Pattern C

From assorted navy prints, cut:
● 2—1½×42" strips
● 8—2⅞" squares, cutting each in half diagonally for a total of 16 triangles
● 1—6½×4½" rectangle

From tan print No. 1, cut:
● 1—1½×42" strip

From tan print No. 2, cut:
● 1—18½×5½" rectangle

From navy plaid, cut:
● 2—2½×31½" border strips
● 2—2½×18½" border strips

From dark navy print, cut:
● 3—2½×42" binding strips

assemble the star block

1. Referring to Diagram 1 for placement, join the cream print 3½×1½" rectangles to opposite sides of the dark red print 3½×1½" rectangle. Press the seam allowances toward the dark red print rectangle. Sew together the pieced stripes and the navy-and-white star print 3½" square to make the stars-and-stripes unit. Press the seam allowance toward the navy-and-white star print.

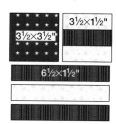

Diagram 1

2. Join the 6½×1½" dark red print rectangles to opposite edges of the cream print 6½×1½" rectangle to make the stripes unit. Press the seam allowances toward the dark red print rectangles. Sew together the stripes unit and stars-and-stripes unit to make the flag unit. Press the seam allowance toward the dark red print stripe. The pieced unit should measure 6½" square, including the seam allowances.

3. Referring to Diagram 2, sew together a gold print B triangle, a dark red print A triangle, and a gold print B reversed triangle to make a star point unit. Press one seam allowance toward the dark red triangle and the other seam allowance toward the gold print triangle. The pieced star point unit should measure 6½" square, including the seam allowances. Repeat to make a total of four star point units.

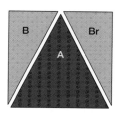

Diagram 2

4. Sew together the tan print 1½×42" strip and a navy print 1½×42" strip to make a strip set (see Diagram 3). Press the seam allowance toward the navy print strip. Cut the strip set into a total of twenty-four 1½"-wide segments.

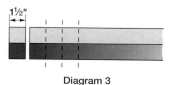

Diagram 3

5. Sew together two 1½" wide segments to make a Four-Patch unit (see Diagram 4 on *page 50*). Press the seam allowances in one direction. The pieced Four-Patch unit should measure 2½" square, including the seam allowances. Repeat to make a total of twelve Four-Patch units.

Diagram 4

6. Referring to Diagram 5 for placement, lay out three Four-Patch units and four navy print triangles in three horizontal rows. Join the pieces in each row. Press the seam allowances toward the triangles. Sew together the rows to make a joined Four-Patch unit. Press the seam allowances in one direction. Repeat to make a total of four joined Four-Patch units.

Diagram 5

7. Referring to Diagram 6 for placement, sew a dark red print triangle to opposite sides of a joined Four-Patch unit to make a floating Four-Patch unit. Press the seam allowances toward the dark red print triangles. The pieced floating Four-Patch unit should measure 6½" square, including the seam allowances. Repeat to make a total of four floating Four-Patch units.

Diagram 6

8. Referring to the Quilt Assembly Diagram, *right* for placement, lay out the flag unit, the star point units, and the floating Four-Patch units in three horizontal rows. Sew together the pieces in each row. Press the seam allowances in one direction, alternating directions with each row. Then join the rows to complete the star block. Press the seam allowances in one direction. The star block should measure 18½" square, including the seam allowances.

assemble the four-patch rows

1. Referring to steps 4 and 5 in Assemble the Star Block, *page 49*, use the dark red print 1½×42" strip and a navy print 1½×42" strip to make a total of 14 dark red-and-navy Four-Patch units. Set aside four of the Four-Patch units.

2. Referring to the Quilt Assembly Diagram for placement, sew together five dark red-and-navy Four-Patch units and four dark red print 2½" squares in a row, alternating the Four-Patch units and squares. Press the seam allowances toward the dark red print squares. The pieced Four-Patch row should measure 18½×2½", including the seam allowances. Repeat to make a second pieced Four-Patch row.

complete the appliqué

1. Referring to the Quilt Assembly Diagram for placement, place the gold print stars in the center of the navy print 6½×4½" rectangle and the two dark red print 6½×4½" rectangles. Fuse the shapes in place. Machine-blanket-stitch around the edges of the stars.

2. Sew together the appliquéd rectangles in a row with the navy print rectangle in the center. Press the seam allowances toward the navy print rectangle. The pieced row should measure 18½×4½", including the seam allowances.

3. Arrange the letters for the word "welcome" on the tan print 18½×5½" rectangle. Fuse the letters in place. Machine-blanket-stitch around the edges of each letter.

assemble the quilt center

1. Referring to the Quilt Assembly Diagram for placement, lay out the pieced Four-Patch rows, the appliquéd rows, and the star block.

2. Join the rows to complete the quilt center. Press the seam allowances in one direction. The pieced quilt center should measure 18½×31½", including the seam allowances.

add the border

1. Sew the navy plaid 2½×31½" border strips to the side edges of the pieced quilt center. Press the seam allowances toward the border.

2. Sew a dark red-and-navy Four-Patch unit to each end of the navy plaid 2½×18½" border strips to make border units. Press the seam allowances toward the navy plaid strips.

3. Sew the pieced border units to the top and bottom edges of the quilt center to complete the quilt top. Press the seam allowances toward the border.

complete the quilt

1. Layer the quilt top, batting, and backing according to the instructions in Quilting Basics, which begins on *page 94*.

2. Quilt as desired. This wall hanging was machine-quilted with outline stitching defining the gold star points, the lettering, and the appliqué foundations. A free-form design was used to machine-quilt the remainder of the wall hanging.

3. Use the dark navy print 2½×42" strips to bind the quilt according to the instructions in Quilting Basics.

Quilt Assembly Diagram

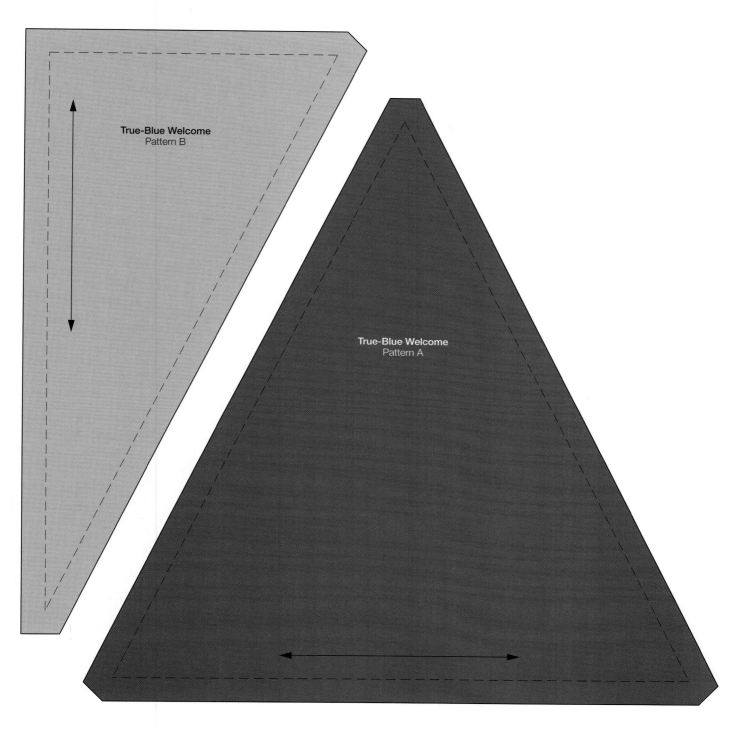

True-Blue Welcome
Pattern B

True-Blue Welcome
Pattern A

Full-Size Patterns

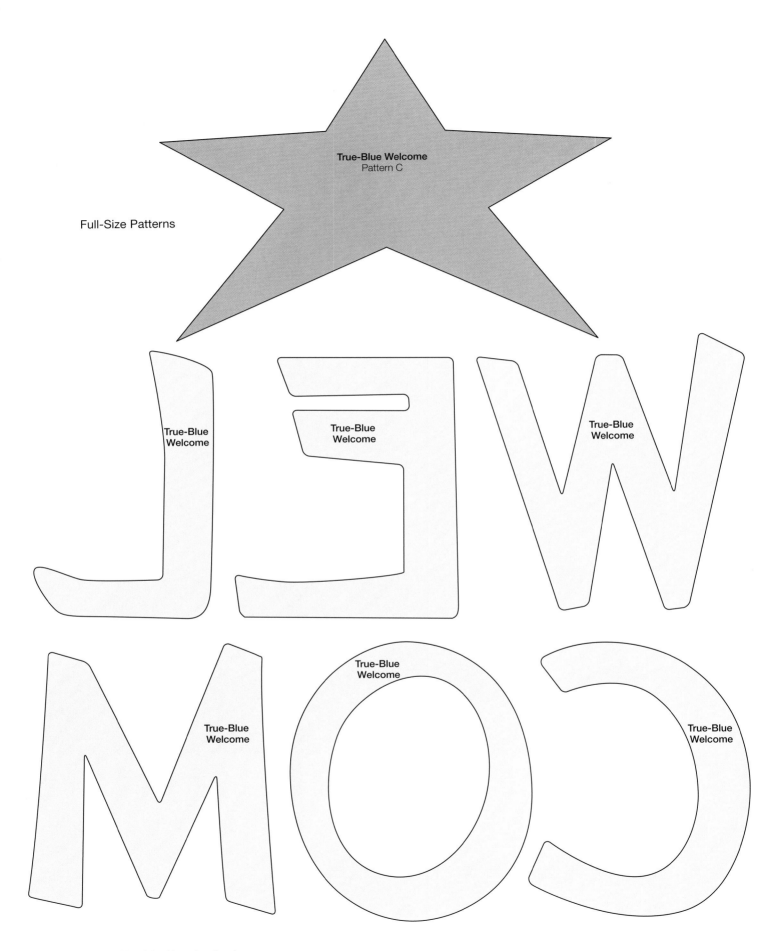

True-Blue Welcome
Pattern C

Full-Size Patterns

True-Blue
Welcome

True-Blue
Welcome

True-Blue
Welcome

True-Blue
Welcome

True-Blue
Welcome

True-Blue
Welcome

mock
hand appliqué

Nearly invisible appliqué stitches don't need to be done by hand. Use our techniques to appliqué your shapes with your sewing machine— and get the same look in a fraction of the time.

emma's
garden

Soft pastel hues and subdued floral prints give this new throw a vintage look. Try stitching the machine-appliquéd shapes with monofilament thread for nearly invisible stitches.

Designer: Linda Hohag   Photographer: Perry Struse

materials

1½ yards of solid cream for appliqué foundations
¼ yard of solid blue for inner border
1⅝ yards of pink print for outer border
¾ yard of pink-and-white check for binding
1 yard total of assorted blue, pink, gold, green, and brown prints for circle and flower appliqués
⅓ yard of assorted dark green prints for calyx appliqués
¼ yard of solid green for leaf and stem appliqués
3¼ yards of backing fabric
58" square of quilt batting
Freezer paper

FINISHED QUILT TOP: 52" square
FINISHED BLOCK: 7" square

Quantities specified for 44/45"-wide, 100% cotton fabrics. All measurements include a ¼" seam allowance. Sew with right sides together unless otherwise stated.

cut the fabrics

To make the best use of your fabrics, cut the pieces in the order that follows. The outer border strips are cut the length of the fabric (parallel to the selvage).

From solid cream, cut:
● 12—8½" squares
● 13—7½" squares
From solid blue, cut:
● 2—1½×37½" inner border strips
● 2—1½×35½" inner border strips
From pink print, cut:
● 2—8×52½" outer border strips
● 2—8×37½" outer border strips

From pink-and-white check, cut:
● 1—26" square, cutting it into enough 2½"-wide bias strips to total 240" in length for binding (For specific instructions on cutting bias strips, see Appliqué Primer, which begins on *page 82*.)

cut and prepare the appliques

The patterns are on *page 57*. The following instructions are for appliquéing with freezer-paper templates. With this technique, freezer paper forms a base around which the fabric is shaped.

1. Trace patterns A through E the number of times indicated onto the dull side of the freezer paper, leaving at least ¼" between tracings. Cut out each freezer-paper template on the traced line.

2. Position the freezer-paper templates, shiny sides down, on the wrong side of the fabrics, leaving ½" between templates. Press the freezer-paper templates in place with a hot, dry iron. Lift the iron after five seconds and check to be sure that each template has completely adhered to the fabric.

3. Cut out each fabric shape, adding a ³⁄₁₆" seam allowance except on Pattern A, which includes seam allowances on the straight sides. (On the curved edge of Pattern A, add the ³⁄₁₆" seam allowance.) Clip the inside curves or points where necessary; do not clip outside curves.

4. Beginning at one inside point, use the tip of a hot, dry iron to fold the seam allowance over the edge of the freezer paper. Continue working around the appliqué shape, folding over one small area at a time and pressing the seam allowance up and over the freezer

paper, except for edges that will be covered by other pieces. Make sure the appliqué fabric is pressed taut against the edges of the freezer paper. Let the appliqué shapes cool, then remove the freezer-paper templates.

From assorted blue, pink, gold, green, and brown prints, cut:
● 52 of Pattern A
● 48 of Pattern B
From assorted dark green prints, cut:
● 48 of Pattern C
From solid green, cut:
● 48 of Pattern D
● 96 of Pattern E

appliqué the blocks

1. Referring to the Quarter-Circle Appliqué Placement Diagram, *below*, place four assorted-color quarter-circle A pieces on a solid cream 7½" square; baste in place. Appliqué the curved edge of each piece as desired to make a quarter-circle block. (**Note:** Using a narrow zigzag stitch, designer Linda Hohag stitched close to the edge of each quarter-circle piece using monofilament thread to make nearly invisible stitches.) Repeat to make a total of 13 quarter-circle blocks.

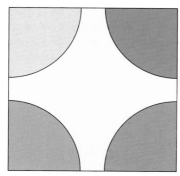

Quarter-Circle Appliqué
Placement Diagram

2. Lightly press the solid cream 8½" squares in half horizontally and vertically to form placement lines; unfold.

3. Referring to the Flower Appliqué Placement Diagram, *below*, position the appliqué pieces for four flowers on a solid cream 8½" square foundation. Align the seam line of each stem (as marked on the pattern) with the raw edge of the foundation; baste. Appliqué the shapes to the foundation. Trim the foundation to 7½" square to make a flower block. Repeat to make a total of 12 flower blocks.

Flower Appliqué Placement Diagram

assemble the quilt center

1. Referring to the photograph at *right* for placement, lay out the 12 flower blocks and the 13 quarter-circle blocks in five horizontal rows, alternating the blocks.

2. Sew together the blocks in each row. Press the seam allowances in one direction, alternating the direction with each row. Then join the rows to make the quilt center. Press the seam allowances in one direction. The pieced quilt center should measure 35½" square, including the seam allowances.

add the borders

1. Sew the solid blue 1½×35½" inner border strips to opposite edges of the pieced quilt center. Then add the solid blue 1½×37½" inner border strips to the remaining edges of the pieced quilt center. Press the seam allowances toward the blue border.

2. Sew the pink print 8×37½" outer border strips to opposite edges of the pieced quilt center. Then add the pink print 8×52½" outer border strips to the remaining edges of the pieced quilt center to complete the quilt top. Press the seam allowances toward the pink print border.

complete the quilt

1. Layer the quilt top, batting, and backing according to the instructions in Quilting Basics, which begins on *page 94*.

2. Quilt as desired. Linda machine-quilted a feather design in the outer border and stipple-quilted the appliqué blocks, adding a flower design to the center of each quarter-circle block.

3. Use Pattern F to mark scallops on the pink print outer border. Trim the border according to the marked scallops.

4. Use the pink-and-white check 2½"-wide bias strips to bind the quilt according to the instructions in Quilting Basics.

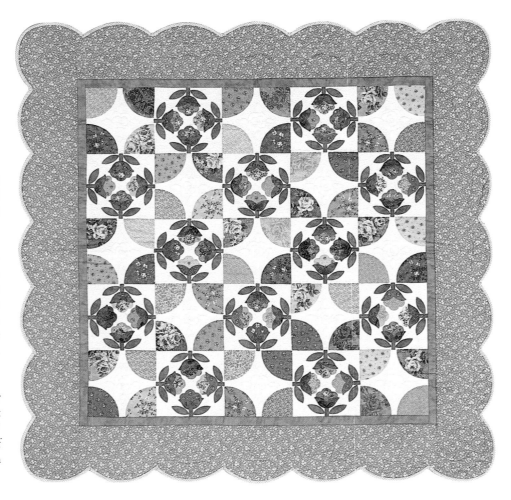

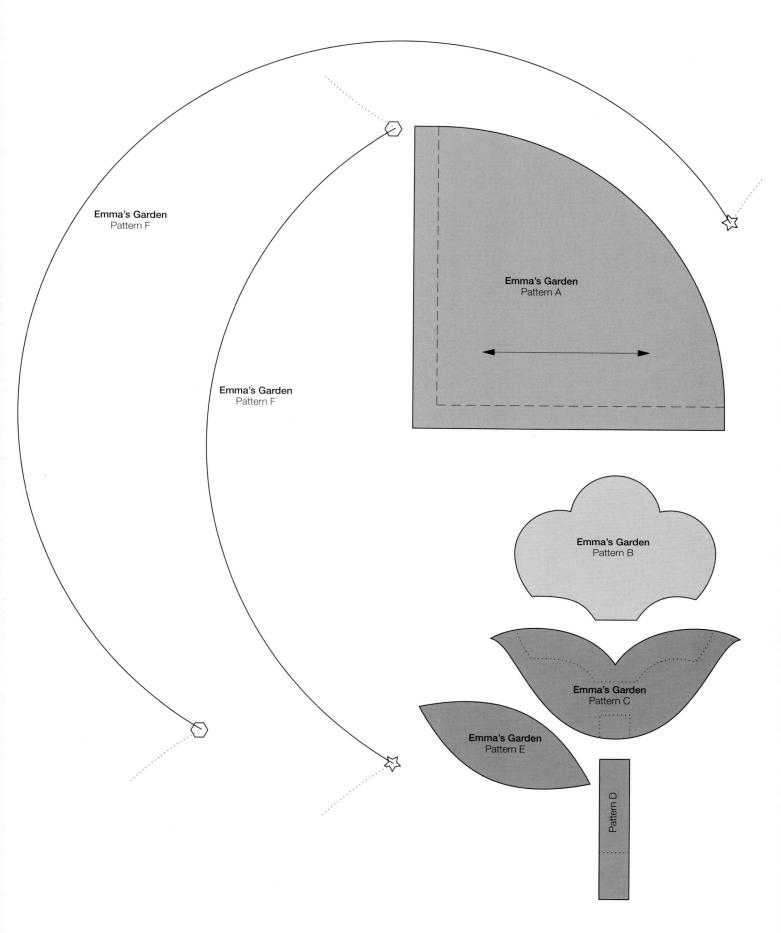

Emma's Garden
Pattern F

Emma's Garden
Pattern F

Emma's Garden
Pattern A

Emma's Garden
Pattern B

Emma's Garden
Pattern C

Emma's Garden
Pattern E

Pattern D

summer
blossoms

Basket blocks frame a center square of appliquéd flowers on this blooming beauty with a background of soft greens.

Designer: Joy Hoffman
Photographer: Perry Struse

materials

1¼ yards of light green print for setting square, setting and corner triangles, outer border, and binding

½ yard of cream print for blocks and inner border

¼ yard of green floral for blocks

¼ yard of pink print for border piping and flower appliqués

½ yard of dark green print for leaf, stem, and vine appliqués

3—⅛-yard pieces of assorted pastel prints in blue, lavender, and peach for flower appliqués

1 yard of backing fabric

36" square of quilt batting

Lightweight muslin interfacing or batiste for appliqué backing (optional)

Quantities specified for 44/45"-wide, 100% cotton fabrics. All measurements include a ¼" seam allowance. Sew with right sides together unless otherwise stated.

FINISHED QUILT TOP: 30¼" square
FINISHED BLOCK: 7½" square

cut the fabrics

To make the best use of your fabrics, cut the pieces in the order that follows. The setting and corner triangles are cut larger than necessary to allow for sewing differences. After assembling the quilt center, you'll trim them to fit.

From light green print, cut:
- 4—4×42" strips for outer border
- 4—2½×42" binding strips
- 1—12¼" square, cutting it diagonally twice in an X for a total of 4 setting triangles
- 2—6½" squares, cutting each diagonally in half to make 4 corner triangles
- 1—8" setting square

From cream print, cut:
- 3—1½×42" strips for inner border
- 8—2×5" rectangles for position D
- 2—5⅜" squares, cutting each diagonally in half to make 4 large triangles for position A

- 2—3⅞" squares, cutting each diagonally in half to make 4 medium triangles for position E
- 12—2⅜" squares, cutting each diagonally in half to make 24 small triangles for position B
- 4—2" squares for position C

From green floral, cut:
- 2—5⅜" squares, cutting each diagonally in half to make 4 large triangles for position A
- 16—2⅜" squares, cutting each diagonally in half to make 32 small triangles for position B

From pink print, cut:
- 4—1×23¾" strips for border piping

From dark green print, cut:
- 1—18" square, cutting it into enough 1¼"-wide strips to cut and piece two strips 36" long, one strip 12" long, and one strip 5" long (For specific instructions on cutting bias strips, see Appliqué Primer, which begins on *page 82*.)

assemble the basket blocks

1. Join a cream print A triangle and a green floral A triangle to make a large triangle-square (see Diagram 1). Press the seam allowance toward the green floral triangle. The pieced large triangle-square should measure 5" square, including the seam allowances.

Diagram 1

2. Repeat Step 1 using a cream print B triangle and a green floral B triangle to make a small triangle-square (see Diagram 2, *above right*). Press the seam allowance toward the green floral triangle. The pieced small triangle-square should measure 2" square, including the seam allowances. Repeat to make a total of six small triangle-squares.

Diagram 2

3. Referring to Diagram 3 for placement, sew together three small triangle-squares in a vertical row. Press the seam allowances in one direction. Sew the vertical row to the right edge of the large triangle-square. Press the seam allowances toward the large triangle-square.

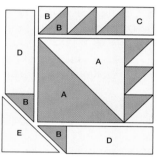

Diagram 3

4. In the same manner, sew together three small triangle-squares and a cream print 2" square in a horizontal row. Press the seam allowances in one direction. Sew the horizontal row to the top edge of the large triangle-square. Press the seam allowances toward the large triangle-square.

5. Pair a green floral B triangle and a cream print D rectangle, noting triangle placement in Diagram 3; sew together. Repeat to make a second pair. Add them to the remaining edges of the large triangle-square. Add a cream print E triangle to the diagonal edge to complete a basket block. The pieced basket block should measure 8" square, including the seam allowances.

6. Repeat steps 1 through 5 to make a total of four basket blocks.

assemble the quilt center

1. Referring to the photograph *opposite* for placement, lay out the four basket blocks, the light green print 8" setting square, and the four light green print setting triangles in diagonal rows. (The four light green print corner triangles will be added later.)

2. Sew together the pieces in each diagonal row. Press the seam allowances toward the light green print pieces; press. Then join the rows. Add the four light green print corner triangles to make the quilt center. Press the seam allowances in one direction.

3. Trim the setting and corner triangles, leaving a ¼" seam allowance beyond the basket block corners. Double-check the corners to make sure they are 90° angles. The pieced quilt center should measure 21¾" square, including the seam allowances.

add the borders

These border strip measurements are mathematically correct. Before cutting, measure your pieced quilt center and adjust the lengths to fit.

1. Cut and piece the cream print 1½×42" strips to make the following:
- 2—1½×23¾" inner border strips
- 2—1½×21¾" inner border strips

2. Sew the short cream print inner border strips to opposite edges of the pieced quilt center. Then add the long cream print inner border strips to the remaining edges of the pieced quilt center. Press the seam allowances toward the border.

3. Fold each pink print 1×23¾" strip in half lengthwise with the wrong sides inside and press. With raw edges aligned, baste the pink print piping strips to opposite edges of the quilt center using a ¼" seam allowance. Then add the pink print piping strips to the remaining edges of the pieced quilt center. Press the seam allowances toward the quilt center.

4. Cut the light green print 4×42" strips to make the following:
- 2—4×30¾" outer border strips
- 2—4×23¾" outer border strips

5. Sew the short light green print outer border strips to opposite edges of the pieced quilt center. Add the long light green print outer border strips to the remaining edges of the pieced quilt center to complete the quilt top.

prepare and add the appliqué pieces

1. Fold the dark green print 1¼×5" bias strip in half lengthwise with the wrong side inside. Using a ⅛" seam allowance, sew down the length of the strip (see Diagram 4). Roll the strip so that the seam is in the middle of one side; press flat to make a stem appliqué. Repeat with the dark green print 12"-long and two 36"-long bias strips to make one stem and two vine appliqués.

Diagram 4

2. Referring to the photograph *opposite*, pin the stems and vines in place on the quilt top. (*Note:* Miter the center of the 12"-long strip to create the two outer stems used in the center setting square; use the 5"-long strip as the center stem.) With dark green thread, machine-appliqué the stems and vines to the quilt top.

3. Lay the lightweight muslin or batiste interfacing over the patterns on *page 61*. With a pencil, trace Pattern A 40 times and Pattern B 59 times, leaving roughly ½" between tracings. Cut out the pieces roughly ¼" outside the traced lines.

Place the interfacing shapes on the right side of the fabrics indicated *below*, leaving ⅜" between shapes; pin in place and cut out, cutting just outside the drawn lines.

From blue print, cut:
- 11 of Pattern A

From lavender print, cut:
- 11 of Pattern A

From peach print, cut:
- 10 of Pattern A

From pink print, cut:
- 8 of Pattern A

From dark green print, cut:
- 59 of Pattern B

4. Stitch together the paired interfacing fabric shapes, sewing on the drawn lines. Trim the seam allowances to ⅛". Clip the inside curves or points on the appliqué shapes where necessary; do not clip the outside curves. Make a small slit in the back of each interfacing piece. Turn the appliqué shapes right side out; press.

5. Referring to the photograph *opposite* for placement, arrange the prepared flower and leaf appliqué shapes on the pieced quilt top; baste.

6. Using coordinating or contrasting threads, machine-stitch the flower appliqués to the quilt top using several decorative stitches at the center of each one. Leave the edges free to give the flower appliqués dimension. Using dark green thread, stitch a line through the center of each dark green leaf appliqué; leave the edges free.

complete the quilt

1. Layer the quilt top, batting, and backing according to the instructions in Quilting Basics, which begins on *page 94*.

2. Quilt as desired. Quilt each appliquéd flower in a crisscross pattern to form petals.

3. Use the light green print 2½×42" strips to bind the quilt according to the instructions in Quilting Basics.

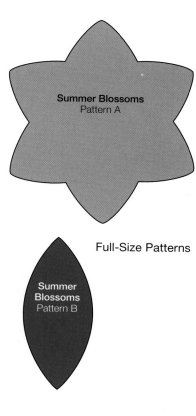

Summer Blossoms
Pattern A

Full-Size Patterns

Summer Blossoms
Pattern B

COLOR OPTION

Plaids—instead of floral prints—give each basket on this autumn-color version a woven appearance. The open spaces surrounding the basket blocks also would make this a great signature quilt.

for the love of licorice

Liquid starch and machine appliqué make working with the curved seams on this red-and-black beauty much easier and faster than doing it by hand.

Designer: Pat Sloan   Photographer: Perry Struse

materials

1½ yards of cream print for blocks
2½ yards of red floral for blocks and outer border
½ yard of red print for blocks
⅓ yard of black print for blocks
⅔ yard of black floral for blocks
⅞ yard of solid black for inner border and binding
3⅝ yards of backing fabric
64×74" of quilt batting
Heat-resistant template plastic
Liquid starch
Cotton swabs

FINISHED QUILT TOP: 58×68"
FINISHED BLOCK: 5" square

Quantities specified for 44/45"-wide, 100% cotton fabrics. All measurements include a ¼" seam allowance. Sew with right sides together unless otherwise stated.

cut the fabrics

To make the best use of your fabrics, cut the pieces in the order that follows. The Wedge Pattern is on *page 65*.

From cream print, cut:
• 40—5½" squares
• 40—4" squares
From red floral, cut:
• 7—8½×42" strips for outer border
• 12—5½" squares
• 16—4" squares
From red print, cut:
• 8—5½" squares
• 4—4" squares
From black print, cut:
• 4—5½" squares
• 8—4" squares
From black floral, cut:

• 16—5½" squares
• 12—4" squares
From solid black, cut:
• 7—2½×42" binding strips
• 5—1½×42" strips for inner border

prepare the wedge appliqués

1. Place the heat-resistant template plastic over the Wedge Pattern. Trace the pattern onto the plastic using a permanent fine-line marker. Cut out on the drawn lines to make the template. Mark the template's right side.

2. Place the template wrong side up on the wrong side of a 4" square, aligning the template's corner with one of the square's corners. Trace the curved edge. Cut the curve, adding a ³⁄₁₆" seam allowance to the curved edge only (see Photo 1). Replace the template on the fabric wedge.

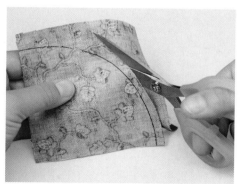
Photo 1

3. Pour a small amount of starch into a dish. Place the template-topped fabric wedge on a pressing surface covered with a tea towel or muslin; make sure the straight edges of the template and fabric wedges are aligned. Dip a cotton swab in the starch and moisten the curved edge's seam allowance (see Photo 2, *above right*).

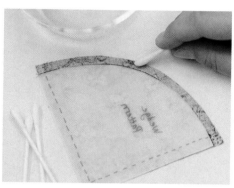
Photo 2

4. Beginning at one end of the curved edge, use the tip of a hot, dry iron to turn the seam allowance over the edge of the template and press it in place until the fabric is dry (see Photo 3).

Photo 3

5. Continue pressing around the curve, adding starch as necessary, to prepare the wedge appliqué. Small pleats in the fabric may appear as you round the curve.

If there is too much bulk in the seam allowance, make small V-shape clips to ease the fabric into place.

6. Turn the template and appliqué over, press the appliqué from the right side, then remove the template.

7. Repeat steps 2 through 6 with all of the cream print, red floral, red print, black print, and black floral 4" squares to make a total of 80 wedge appliqués.

appliqué the blocks

Note: *Contrasting thread is used in these diagrams for illustration purposes only.*

1. With straight edges aligned and right sides facing up, place a red print wedge appliqué atop a cream print 5½" square (see Diagram 1).

Diagram 1

2. Position the pieces on the machine so that the needle will first go into the square right next to the wedge appliqué. The needle should be so near the fold of the wedge appliqué that the needle touches the fold but does not stitch through it (see Diagram 2).

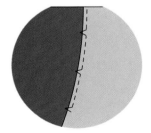

Diagram 2

When the needle jumps to the left as the first part of the zigzag stitch, the needle should be totally on the wedge appliqué.

When the needle jumps to the right to complete the zigzag stitch, the needle should again be touching the fold but stitching only through the square foundation.

3. Continue stitching along the curved edge of the wedge appliqué until it's completely stitched to the square (see Diagram 3).

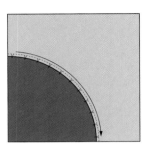

Diagram 3

4. Check the curved edge of the wedge appliqué to make sure no areas were left unstitched. On the wrong side, carefully trim away the square fabric from behind the wedge appliqué, leaving a ¼" seam allowance (see Diagram 4) to make a block.

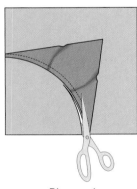

Diagram 4

5. Place a thick bath towel atop your pressing surface and lay the appliquéd block facedown on the towel. Cover the block with a pressing cloth; press with a warm iron. (The towel prevents edges of the appliqué from being flattened by the iron.)

6. Repeat steps 1 through 5, appliquéing the remaining red print, red floral, black print, and black floral wedges onto the remaining cream print 5½" squares, and appliquéing the cream print wedges onto the red print, red floral, black print, and black floral 5½" squares to make a total of 80 appliquéd blocks.

assemble the quilt center

1. Referring to the Quilt Assembly Diagram *opposite* and the photograph on *page 62* for placement, arrange the 80 appliquéd blocks in 10 horizontal rows.

2. Sew together the blocks in each row. Press the seam allowances in one direction, alternating the direction with each row. Then join the rows to make the quilt center. Press the seam allowances in one direction. The pieced quilt center should measure 40½×50½", including the seam allowances.

add the borders

1. Cut and piece the solid black 1½×42" strips to make the following:
- 2—1½×50½" inner border strips
- 2—1½×42½" inner border strips

2. Sew the long solid black inner border strips to the side edges of the pieced quilt center. Then join the short solid black inner border strips to the top and bottom edges of the quilt center. Press all seam allowances toward the inner border.

3. Cut and piece the red floral 8½×42" strips to make the following:
- 2—8½×58½" outer border strips
- 2—8½×52½" outer border strips

4. Sew the short red floral outer border strips to the side edges of the quilt center. Then join the long red floral outer border strips to the top and bottom edges of the quilt center to complete the quilt top. Press all seam allowances toward the outer border.

complete the quilt

1. Layer the quilt top, batting, and backing according to the instructions in Quilting Basics, which begins on *page 94*. Quilt as desired.

2. Use the solid black 2½×42" strips to bind the quilt according to the instructions in Quilting Basics.

setting up your machine

Install a new size 60/8, 70/10, or 75/11 embroidery needle in your sewing machine.

Wind a bobbin with 60-weight cotton embroidery thread.

Thread the needle with lightweight, invisible, nylon (monofilament) thread. Use clear thread for light-color fabrics; use smoke-color invisible thread for medium- and dark-color fabrics.

Set your machine for a blind hemstitch with the stitch width and length each set at 1 mm. This means your machine will take two to five straight stitches, then a zigzag stitch, then two to five more straight stitches before zigzagging again. Stitch a test sample before stitching actual quilt pieces.

COLOR OPTION
Stitched in flannels, this unique version of the quilt shows what can happen by simply rotating the blocks. While flannel can be more difficult to work with, especially when sewing curves, the liquid-starch appliqué technique makes this an easy block to sew.

Quilt Assembly Diagram

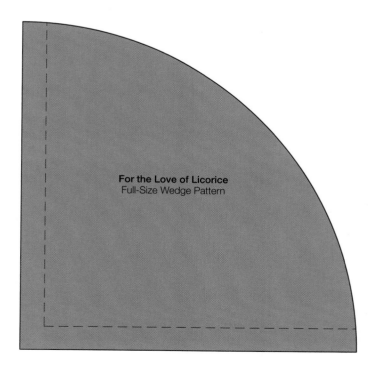

For the Love of Licorice
Full-Size Wedge Pattern

decorative-stitch
appliqué

Use your sewing machine's decorative stitch capabilities to enhance your appliqué motifs. Zigzag, straight, and free-motion stitches in eye-catching colored threads are just a few of the options.

Surprise someone special with a card that you can stitch with your own personalized greeting. Cut out the shapes from fabric scraps and use fusing-adhesive material to make each of these small gifts in no time.

Designer: Terri Pauser Wolf
Photographer: Perry Struse

greeting cards

materials

Assorted fabrics
Assorted threads
Rotary cutter with specialty blades, such
   as wavy and pinking
Acrylic frame
Batting scraps
Rubber stamp letters and fabric ink pad
   or fabric marking pen
Lightweight fusible web

cut the fabrics

1. Measure your acrylic frame.

2. For the appliqué foundation and the backing, cut two fabric pieces 1" larger than the frame on all sides. Cut another fabric piece that is half the height and the same width as the backing piece to serve as the sleeve on the back. Cut enough ½"-wide strips for binding.

prepare the appliqués

1. Designer Terri Pauser Wolf likes to make each of her cards unique. She usually cuts the appliqué shapes freehand for each card. For freehand cutting, lay the fusible web, paper side up, on the wrong side of assorted fabric pieces; fuse and let cool. Cut the fabrics, using specialty blades if desired. Cut out desired individual shapes, letters, or words.

2. If you wish to use patterns in making your cards, see *opposite* for assorted appliqué shapes. To make templates of the patterns, follow the instructions in Appliqué Primer, which begins on *page 82*. When cutting out the pattern pieces, leave a ½" space between tracings; cut out ¼" away from the traced lines. Following the manufacturer's instructions, press the fusible web shapes onto the backs of fabrics; let cool. Cut out the appliqué fabric shapes on the drawn lines, using specialty blades if desired. Peel off the paper backing.

create a card

1. Arrange the appliqué shapes on the appliqué foundation. When pleased with the arrangement, fuse the pieces in place according to the manufacturer's instructions to make the card top.

2. Thread your machine, both top and bobbin, with thread that either contrasts or coordinates with your fabrics. Attach a free-motion quilting or darning foot to your machine and drop the feed dogs. (*Note:* If your machine cannot drop its feed dogs, tape a business card or other stiff paper over them to prevent them from "grabbing" the fabric.)

3. Layer the appliquéd card top, batting, and backing; baste. Using threads in a variety of colors, free-motion machine-quilt over the appliqués to anchor them in place. Embellish the background as desired.

complete a card

1. Trim the quilted card to straighten the edges, leaving a margin of at least ¼" along all sides. This will make the quilted card ½" longer and wider than the height and width of the chosen frame. For example, a quilted card for an 8×10" frame should measure 8½×10½" at this point.

2. Press under ¼" along the edge of the sleeve that won't be covered by the binding; stitch in place. Place the sleeve, right side up, on the backing; pin, making sure the outer edges are aligned with the card edges so they will be caught in the binding.

3. Use the ½"-wide strips to bind the card according to the instructions in Quilting Basics, which begins on *page 94*.

4. Slide the quilted card over the acrylic frame.

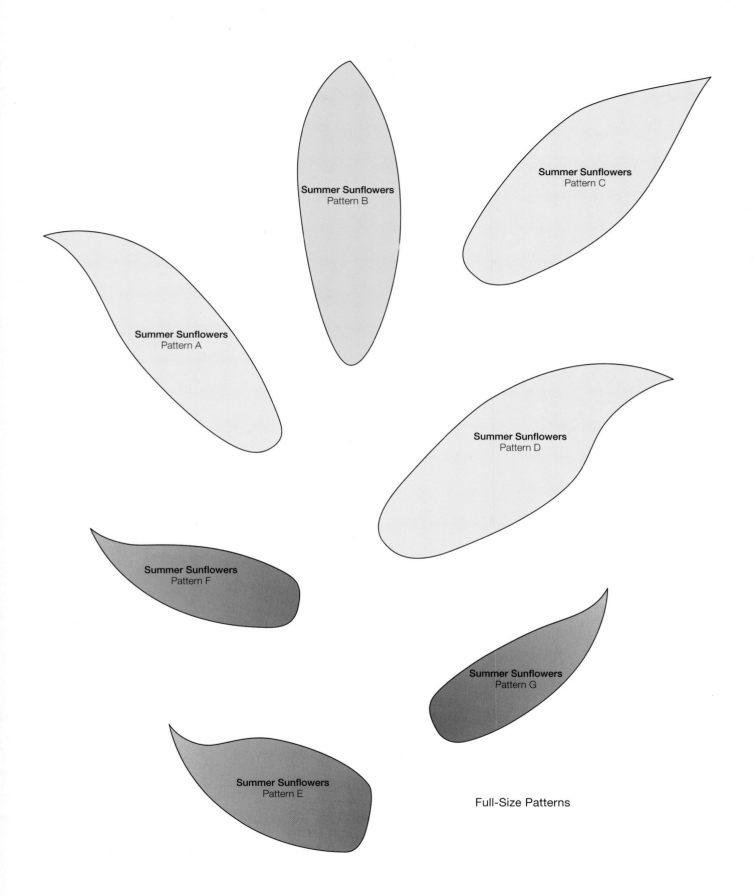

Summer Sunflowers
Pattern B

Summer Sunflowers
Pattern C

Summer Sunflowers
Pattern A

Summer Sunflowers
Pattern D

Summer Sunflowers
Pattern F

Summer Sunflowers
Pattern G

Summer Sunflowers
Pattern E

Full-Size Patterns

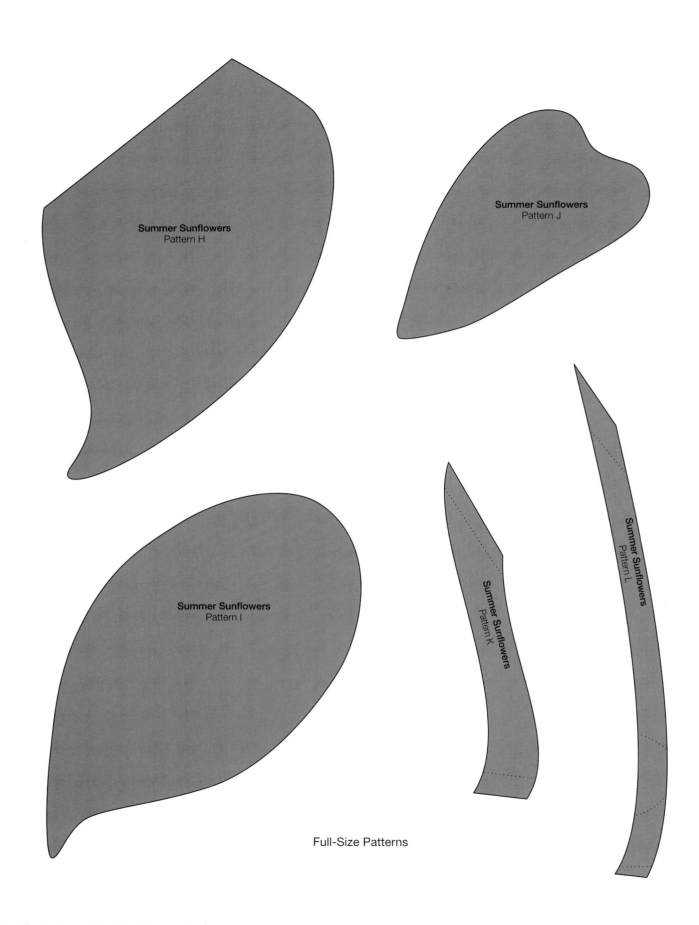

Summer Sunflowers
Pattern H

Summer Sunflowers
Pattern J

Summer Sunflowers
Pattern I

Summer Sunflowers
Pattern K

Summer Sunflowers
Pattern L

Full-Size Patterns

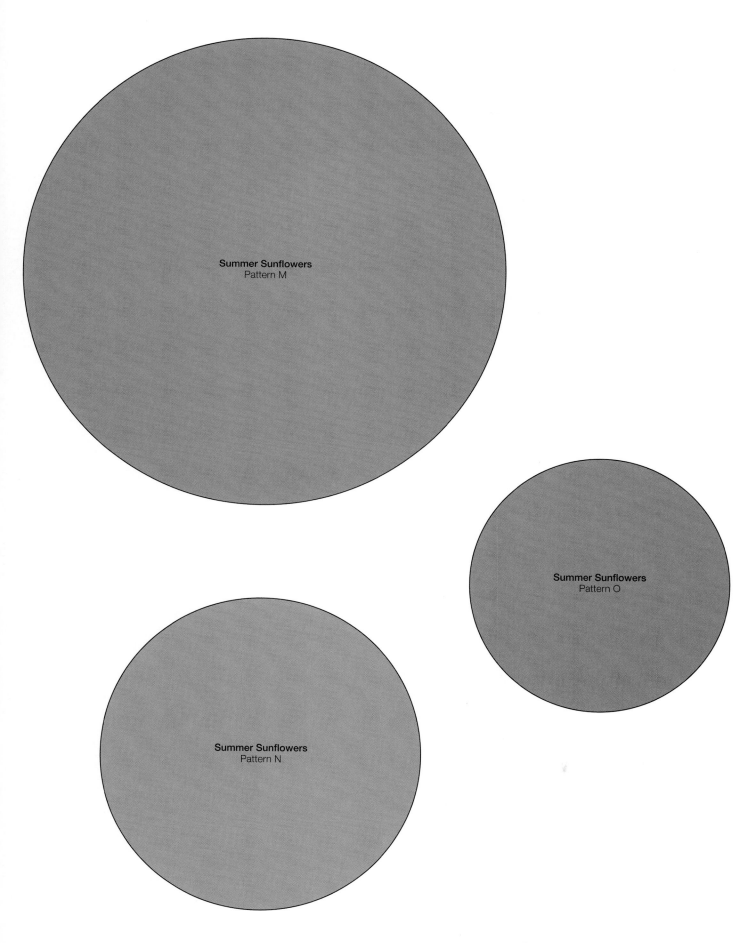

Summer Sunflowers
Pattern M

Summer Sunflowers
Pattern O

Summer Sunflowers
Pattern N

wild roses

Although the design looks complicated, this appliqué trellis of roses is created using basic stitches found on most sewing machines. Hand-dyed fabrics add to the effect of realism.

Designer: Janet Pittman   Photographer: Perry Struse

materials

½ yard of light green print for appliqué
  foundation
¼ yard of beige print for fence appliqué
14" square of green print for leaf
  appliqués
9" square of red print for petal appliqués
12" square of dark red print for petal
  appliqués
2" square of pink print for rose center
  appliqués
⅓ yard of dark green print for border and
  binding
22×30" of backing fabric
22×30" of quilt batting
1 yard of lightweight fusible web
Embroidery stabilizer
Machine-appliqué thread (40-weight
  rayon or 50-weight cotton thread in
  matching or accenting colors for
  appliqué)

FINISHED QUILT TOP: 16×24"

Quantities specified for 44/45"-wide, 100%
cotton fabrics. All measurements include a
¼" seam allowance. Sew with right sides
together unless otherwise stated.

cut the fabrics

To make the best use of your fabrics, cut the
pieces in the order that follows.

The patterns are on *pages 80–81.* To use
fusible web for appliquéing, as was done in
this project, complete the following steps.

1. Lay the fusible web, paper side up, over
the patterns. Use a pencil to trace the
patterns the number of times indicated,
leaving ½" between tracings. Cut out each
piece roughly ¼" outside the traced lines.
Cut ¼" inside the traced lines of each piece
and discard the centers.

2. Following the manufacturer's instructions,
press the fusible-web shapes onto the backs
of the designated fabrics; let cool. Cut out
the shapes on the drawn lines. Peel off the
paper backings.

From light green print, cut:
- 1—13×21" rectangle for appliqué
  foundation

From beige print, cut:
- 3—2×18" rectangles
- 1—2×14" rectangle

From green print, cut:
- 4 of Pattern A
- 17 of Pattern B
- 16 of Pattern C
- 3 of Pattern D

From red print, cut:
- 1 *each* of patterns E, F, G, H, and I

From dark red print, cut:
- 2 *each* of patterns J, K, L, M, N,
  O, P, and Q
- 3 of Pattern R

From pink print, cut:
- 2 of Pattern S

From dark green print, cut:
- 3—1½×42" binding strips
- 2—2½×20½" border strips
- 2—2½×16½" border strips

appliqué the quilt center

1. Stack the three beige 2×18" rectangles
atop one another. At one short end, mark the
center. Measure and mark 2" down from each
corner. Connect the center mark with each
side mark; trim the end to a point by cutting
on the drawn lines (see Diagram 1, *above
right*). Separate the rectangles into three
fence pickets.

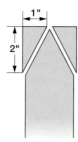

Diagram 1

2. Referring to Diagram 2 for placement,
place the three beige fence pickets on
the light green print 13×21" appliqué
foundation, staggering the heights; pin in
place. Add the beige print 2×14" rectangle
diagonally across the pickets as shown; pin
in place.

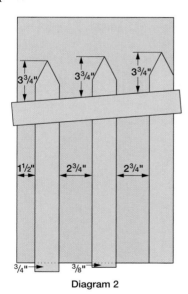

Diagram 2

3. Stitch the edges of the fence pieces to the
foundation with a short, narrow zigzag stitch
(1.5 mm wide and .75 to 1-mm long) to
make the quilt center.

4. Referring to the Appliqué Placement Diagram, *below right,* for placement, arrange the appliqué pieces on the quilt center. When you are pleased with the arrangement, fuse the shapes in place.

5. Using a 3-mm-wide blind hem stitch or vari-overlock stitch, matching thread, and a stabilizer beneath the area being stitched, machine-stitch around the leaves with the points of the stitch extending about ⅛" beyond the leaf edge. *Note:* Designer Janet Pittman likes to position the appliqué foundation in an embroidery hoop to keep it taut as she is machine-stitching it.

Use the same thread to machine-zigzag-stitch around the edges of the Pattern D bud casings.

6. Use a 1-mm-wide, .5-mm-long zigzag stitch and brown-green thread to machine-stitch the leaf veins.

For the stems, place a piece of stabilizer beneath the area being stitched. Use the same thread to machine-stitch the leaf stems with a 1.5-mm-wide satin stitch setting; stitch the larger stems with a 2-mm-wide setting.

7. Using a 1.5-mm-wide satin stitch and red thread, machine-stitch around the flower petals. *Note:* If your machine has a continuously variable zigzag width adjustment, increase the stitch width on the outer edges of the petals and decrease it as you near the center.

8. Using a machine-set triple stitch, stitch wood grain on the fence pieces using a beige, then taupe thread. *Note:* If your machine does not have a triple stitch, straight-stitch two or three rows of stitching, one on top of the next.

9. Using two shades of yellow thread, free-motion machine-stitch a pistil and stamen in the center of each flower, almost completely covering the pink center.

Appliqué Placement Diagram

add the border

1. Trim the appliquéd quilt center to measure 12½×20½", including the seam allowances.

2. Sew the dark green print 2½×20½" border strips to the side edges of the appliquéd quilt center. Press the seam allowances toward the dark green print border.

3. Sew the dark green print 2½×16½" border strips to the top and bottom edges of the appliquéd quilt center to complete the quilt top. Press the seam allowances toward the dark green print border.

complete the quilt

1. Layer the quilt top, batting, and backing according to the instructions in Quilting Basics, which begins on *page 94*.

2. Using monofilament thread, quilt around each appliqué piece, the leaf veins, and some of the fence wood grain. Stipple the quilt center with the small leaf and vines shapes. With green thread, quilt the border with rose leaf shapes.

3. The binding on this quilt only shows on the quilt back. Follow the instructions in Quilting Basics to prepare the dark green print 1½×42" strips for binding. Stitch the prepared binding strips on the quilt top with a ¼" seam allowance, pivoting at the corners instead of making a mitered fold. Fold all of the binding to the back, so the seam line where the binding and quilt top meet is on the outer quilt edge, and stitch by hand.

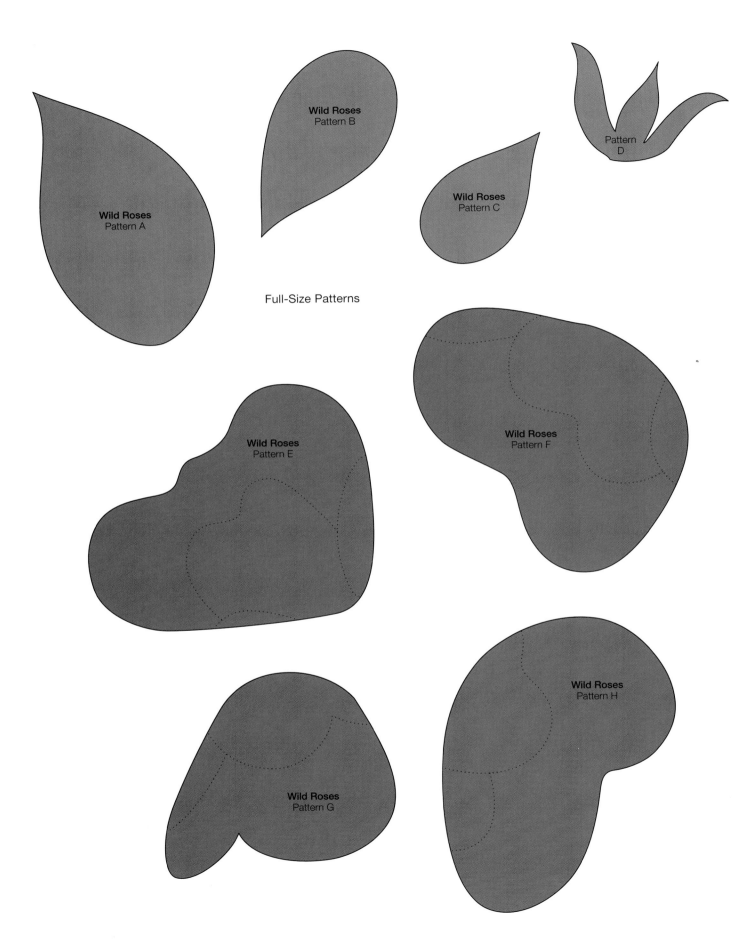

Wild Roses
Pattern A

Wild Roses
Pattern B

Wild Roses
Pattern C

Pattern
D

Full-Size Patterns

Wild Roses
Pattern E

Wild Roses
Pattern F

Wild Roses
Pattern G

Wild Roses
Pattern H

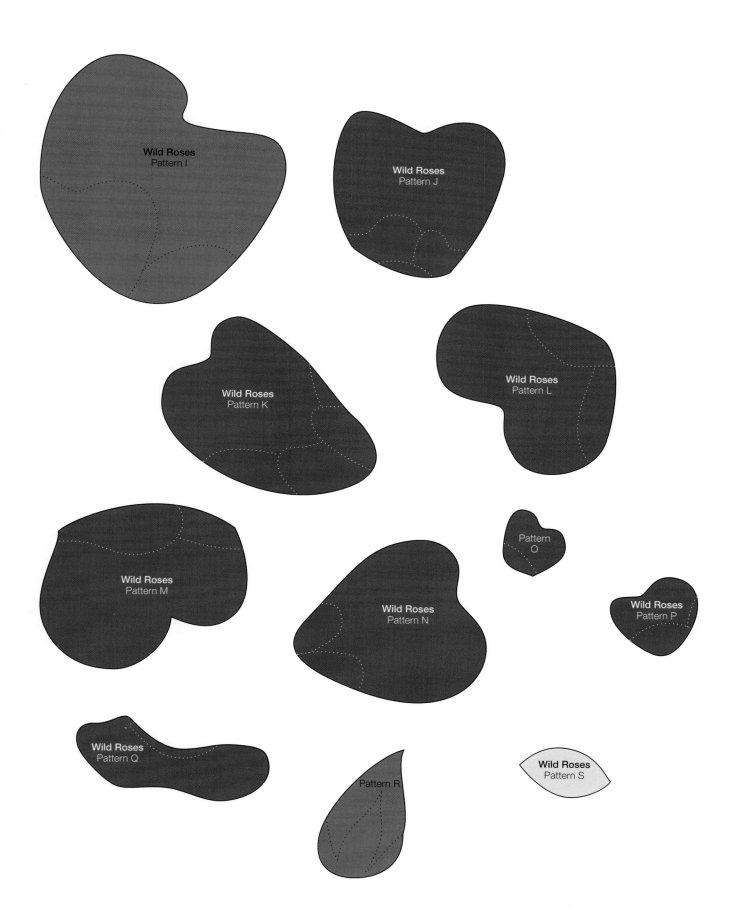

Wild Roses
Pattern I

Wild Roses
Pattern J

Wild Roses
Pattern K

Wild Roses
Pattern L

Wild Roses
Pattern M

Wild Roses
Pattern N

Pattern O

Wild Roses
Pattern P

Wild Roses
Pattern Q

Pattern R

Wild Roses
Pattern S

appliqué primer

The time-honored tradition of appliqué—adding fabric motifs to a foundation fabric—allows for freedom in design not always available with piecing. Styles range from simple to intricate, primitive to elegant. Appliqué can be done by hand or machine. Numerous appliqué methods have been developed, giving quiltmakers lots of choices for the finished appearance.

templates

An appliqué template is a pattern used to trace the appliqué shape onto fabric. The template's material depends on how often the template will be used. Make sure that your template will hold up to the wear that it receives from multiple tracings without deteriorating at the edges. A sturdy, durable material such as template plastic, available at quilt and crafts supply stores, is suitable for making permanent templates for scissors-cut appliqué pieces.

making appliqué templates

1. For most appliqué techniques you need to make your templates the exact size of the finished pieces with no seam allowances included. The seam allowances are added when you cut out the appliqué fabric shapes. Trace the patterns onto template plastic using a permanent marker. Use a ruler for any straight lines.

2. Mark each appliqué template with its letter designation, grain line (if indicated), block name, and appliqué sequence order. Mark an X on edges that do not need to be turned under and transfer the Xs to the fabric shapes when you trace around the templates.

3. Cut out each template, then verify its accuracy by placing it over its printed patterns.

using appliqué templates

1. Choose a marking tool to trace around the templates on fabric. A pencil works well on light-color fabric; a white, silver, or yellow dressmaker's pencil is a good choice on dark-color fabric. If you're using a pencil, keep the point sharp to ensure accuracy. Do not use a ballpoint or ink pen; it may bleed when washed. Test all marking tools on a fabric scrap before using them.

2. Place templates on the fabric, positioning them at least ½" apart. (Whether you place them faceup or facedown on the fabric's right or wrong side depends on the appliqué method you choose.) Trace around each template with your selected marking tool. The drawn lines represent the sewing lines. The specific appliqué technique you choose will dictate how much, if any, seam allowance you leave when cutting out the shape.

3. Cut out the appliqué shapes, including seam allowances if necessary for your chosen appliqué method.

stitching sequence

Edges of appliqué pieces that will be covered by other pieces do not need to be turned under before they are appliquéd. By preparing all your appliqué pieces at one time, you can plan any overlaps, which will save stitching time and considerable bulk in the finished project.

If your pattern does not indicate a numerical stitching sequence, observe which piece is closest to the foundation fabric and farthest away from you. That is the first piece you should appliqué to the foundation. Appliqué the rest of the pieces to the foundation, working from the bottom layer to the top.

prepare appliqué pieces

Prepare your appliqué pieces according to the needs of your chosen appliqué method. Preparation options include basting, freezer paper, spray starch, double appliqué, and fusible web. Read the introduction to each method that follows to determine which one will work best for your selected project.

basting method

This method uses a reusable template, marking tool, and thread to prepare appliqué pieces for hand or machine appliqué.

 **1.** Place your templates on the right side of the fabric, positioning them at least ½" apart; trace.

 **2.** Cut out the appliqué shapes, adding a ³⁄₁₆" seam allowance to all edges. Clip inside curves and points to within a thread of the marked lines, making clips closer together in the curved areas. Try to make your clips on the bias grain of the seam allowance, which means the clips often will be diagonal, rather than perpendicular, lines. This directional clipping prevents fabric from raveling while you're working with the edges.

 **3.** Working from the right side of the appliqué piece and beginning at an inner point, use a contrasting-color thread to baste the seam allowance under following the marked lines. For easier removal of the thread later, begin and end your basting thread on the right side of the appliqué piece.

 **4.** For a sharp outer point, fold the fabric straight over the point.

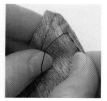 **5.** Then fold in an adjacent seam allowance, overlapping the folded point. Baste in place.

 **6.** As you reach the outer point, fold over the remaining adjacent seam allowance and continue basting around the shape.

using freezer paper

Many quilters choose to use freezer paper for appliqué. Available in grocery stores and some quilt shops, freezer paper has a shiny coating on one side that temporarily adheres to fabric when pressed with a warm iron. It is not necessary to consider the grain line of the fabric when utilizing freezer-paper templates.

freezer-paper method 1

This method uses freezer-paper templates to hold the seam allowances of the appliqué pieces in place. (Refer to Using Freezer Paper, above, for additional information.) This technique may be used to prepare pieces for hand or machine appliqué.

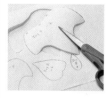 **1.** Trace the appliqué patterns on the dull side of the freezer paper. Cut out the shapes on the traced lines to make freezer-paper templates.

 2. Place the freezer-paper templates dull side up on the right side of the fabric. While holding the freezer paper in place, cut the shapes from the fabric, adding a ³⁄₁₆" seam allowance to all edges.

 **3.** Turn the freezer-paper templates shiny side up and place on the wrong side of the appliqué shape. Clip the inside curves or points on the appliqué shapes. When clipping inside curves, clip halfway through the seam allowances. Try to make your clips on the bias grain of the seam allowance, which means the clips often will be diagonal, rather than perpendicular, lines. This

directional clipping prevents fabric from raveling while you're working with the edges.

 **4.** Beginning at an inner point of an appliqué shape, use the tip of a hot, dry iron to push the seam allowance over the edge of the freezer paper. The seam allowance will adhere to the shiny side of the freezer paper. **Note:** Do not touch the iron soleplate to the freezer paper past the turned fabric edge.

 **5.** Continue working around the appliqué shape, turning one small area at a time and pressing the seam allowance up and over the freezer paper. Make certain the appliqué fabric is pressed taut against the freezer-paper template.

Small pleats in the fabric may appear as you round the outer curves. If there is too much bulk in a seam allowance, make small V clips around the outer curves to ease the fabric around the edge.

 **6.** For a sharp outer point, fold the fabric straight over the point of the freezer-paper template; press to the freezer paper.

 **7.** With the tip of the iron, push an adjacent seam allowance over the edge of the freezer paper. Repeat with the remaining adjacent seam allowance, pushing the seam allowance taut to ensure a sharp point.

 **8.** After all edges are pressed, let the appliqué shape cool, then either remove the freezer-paper template before proceeding with the desired hand- or machine-appliqué technique or leave it in to stitch.

freezer-paper method 2

This technique involves pressing entire freezer-paper templates shiny side down to the appliqué fabric. The freezer paper is removed before the appliqué is sewn in place. This technique may be used to prepare pieces for hand or machine appliqué.

1. Trace a reverse image of the appliqué patterns on the dull side of the freezer paper. Cut out the shapes on the traced lines to make freezer-paper templates. *Note:* To create a reverse image, tape the appliqué pattern facedown on a light box or a sunny window.

2. Place the appliqué fabric wrong side up on a pressing surface. With a dry iron on a cotton setting, press a freezer-paper shape shiny side down to the appliqué fabric. Leave the iron on the paper for a few seconds. Lift the iron to check that the template is completely adhered to the fabric. If the template is not completely adhered, press again.

3. Cut out the appliqué shape, adding a ³⁄₁₆" seam allowance to all edges. Clip inside curves or points on the appliqué shape. When clipping inside curves, clip halfway through the seam allowance. Try to make your clips on the bias grain of the seam allowance, which means the clips often will be on diagonal, rather than perpendicular, lines. This directional clipping prevents fabric from raveling while you're working with the edges.

4. Beginning at one inner point of an appliqué shape, use the tip of a dry, hot iron to push the seam allowance over the edge of the freezer paper to create a sharp edge. *Note:* The seam allowance will not adhere to the dull side of the freezer paper.

5. Continue working around the appliqué shape, turning one small area at a time and pressing the seam allowance up and over the freezer paper. Make certain the appliqué fabric is pressed taut against the edges of the freezer-paper template.

Small pleats in the fabric may appear as you round the outer curves. If there is too much bulk in a seam allowance, make small V clips around the outer curves to ease the fabric around the edge.

6. For a sharp outer point, fold the fabric straight over the point of the freezer-paper template; press.

7. With the tip of the iron, push an adjacent seam allowance over the edge of the freezer paper. Repeat with the remaining adjacent seam allowance, pushing the seam allowance taut to ensure a sharp point.

8. After all the edges are pressed, let the appliqué shape cool, then remove the freezer-paper template.

freezer-paper method 3

This method involves pressing entire freezer-paper templates shiny side down to the appliqué fabric. A water-soluble glue stick is used to hold the seam allowances in place. The freezer paper is not removed until after the appliqué is sewn in place. (Refer to Using Freezer Paper on page 83 for additional information.)

1. Trace a reverse image of the appliqué patterns onto the dull side of the freezer paper. Cut out the shapes on the traced lines to make freezer-paper templates. *Note:* To create a reverse image, tape the appliqué pattern facedown on a light box or a sunny window.

2. Place the appliqué fabric wrong side up on a pressing surface. With a dry iron on a cotton setting, press a freezer-paper template shiny side down to the appliqué fabric. Leave the iron on the paper for a few seconds. Lift the iron to check that the template is completely adhered to the fabric. If the template is not completely adhered, press again.

3. Cut out the appliqué shape, adding a ³⁄₁₆" seam allowance to all edges. Clip the inside curves or points on the appliqué shape. To make a sharp edge at a deep inside point, clip the seam allowance to within one thread of the freezer-paper template.

When clipping the inside curves, cut halfway through the seam allowance. Try to make your clips on the bias grain of the seam allowance, which means the clips will be diagonal, rather than perpendicular, lines. This directional clipping prevents fabric from raveling while you're working with the edges.

4. Using a water-soluble glue stick, apply glue to the exposed seam allowance and the outer edge of the freezer-paper template.

5. At a deep inside point, use the tip of your thumb to press the seam allowance on both sides of the clip down against the freezer-paper template.

Small pleats in the fabric may appear as you round outer curves. If there is too much bulk in the seam allowance, make small V clips around the outer curves to ease the fabric around the edge.

6. Using the tips of your thumb and index finger, continue working the seam allowance over the edge by pinching the fabric. Work in small areas at a time.

7. To make a sharp outer point, fold and glue the fabric point straight over the point of the freezer-paper template. Push one adjacent edge of the seam allowance over the edge of the freezer paper; glue. Repeat with the remaining adjacent seam allowance.

8. The freezer-paper template is not removed until after the appliqué is stitched in place (see About Stabilizers on page 89 for information on removing templates after you've sewn the appliqué in place).

TIP: Store your glue sticks in the refrigerator. This keeps them firmer, making them easier to use and longer lasting.

spray-starch method

With this method, spray starch holds the appliqué's seam allowances against a reusable, heat-resistant template, which you remove before you sew the appliqué in place. This technique may be used to prepare pieces for hand or machine appliqué.

1. Make a heat-resistant plastic template the exact finished size of the appliqué motif. Mark the template's right side.

2. Place the template wrong side up on the wrong side of the appliqué fabric and trace it. Cut around the shape, adding a 3/16" seam allowance to all edges.

3. With wrong sides up, center the template on the appliqué fabric shape. Spray a small amount of starch into a dish. Working on a pressing surface covered with a tea towel or muslin, dip a cotton swab in the starch and moisten the outer edge of the seam allowance.

4. Clip all the inside points. Beginning at an inside point, use the tip of a hot, dry iron to turn the seam allowance over the edge of the template and press it in place until the fabric is dry.

5. Continue pressing around the appliqué shape, clipping the inside curves or points and adding starch as necessary. When clipping the inside curves, cut halfway through the seam allowance. Try to make your clips on the bias grain of the seam allowance, which means the clips often will be diagonal, rather than perpendicular, lines. This directional clipping prevents fabric from raveling while you're working with the edges. Make certain the fabric is pressed taut against the appliqué template.

6. To make a sharp outer point, moisten the seam allowance and fold the fabric point straight over the point of the plastic template. Push one adjacent edge of the seam allowance over the edge of the plastic. Repeat with the remaining adjacent seam allowance.

Small pleats in the fabric may appear as you round the outer curves. If there is too much bulk in the seam allowance, make small V clips around outer curves to ease the fabric around the edge.

7. Press the appliqué from the right side and remove the template.

double-appliqué method

This method eases the challenge of turning under seam allowances by facing the appliqué pieces with sheer, featherweight, nonfusible, nonwoven interfacing. This technique may be used to prepare pieces for hand or machine appliqué.

1. Place a rigid template wrong side up on the wrong side of the appliqué fabric; trace. The traced line is your stitching line.

2. With right sides together, layer your appliqué fabric with a like-size piece of sheer, featherweight, nonfusible, nonwoven interfacing.

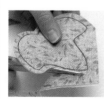

3. Sew the pieces together, stitching on the marked line. Cut out the appliqué shape, adding a 3/16" allowance to all edges.

4. Trim the interfacing seam allowance slightly smaller than the appliqué fabric. This will enable the seam allowance to roll slightly to the back side

of the appliqué once it is turned. Clip at the inner curves and points.

5. Clip a small slit in the center of the interfacing, being careful not to cut through the appliqué fabric.

6. Turn the appliqué right side out through the slit.

7. Press the appliqué piece from the right side.

fusible-web method

Manufacturer's instructions for adhering fusible web vary by brand. Follow the instructions that come with your fusible web to ensure success. Factors such as the iron's temperature setting, a dry or steam iron, and the length of time you press are critical to attaining a secure bond between the fusible web and the fabric. This method eliminates the need to turn under any seam allowances. Choose a lightweight, paper-backed fusible web that can be stitched through unless you plan to leave the appliqué edges unfinished. If the appliqué edges will not be sewn in place, you may wish to use a heavyweight, no-sew fusible web. This technique is commonly used for machine appliqué but also can be used for hand appliqué.

1. Position the fusible web with the paper side up over the appliqué patterns and place them on a light box. Use a pencil to trace each pattern the number of times specified. If you are tracing multiple pieces at one time, leave at least ½" between tracings. **Note:** If you are not using an appliqué pattern designed especially for fusible web, you will need to create a mirror image of the pattern before tracing it. If you don't, your appliqués will be reversed once you cut them from fabric. To create a reverse image, tape the appliqué pattern facedown on a light box or a sunny window.

Cut out the traced appliqué patterns roughly ¼" outside the traced lines. Do not cut directly on the traced lines.

2. If you are working with multiple appliqué layers or want to reduce the stiffness of the finished project, consider cutting away the center of your fusible-web shapes. To do this, cut ¼" inside the traced lines and discard the centers.

3. Place the fusible-web shapes paper side up on the back of the designated appliqué fabrics. Press in place following the manufacturer's instructions. Do not slide the iron, but pick it up to move it from one area to the next. Let the appliqué shapes cool.

4. Cut out the fabric shapes on the drawn lines. Peel off the paper backings.

make bias stems

Fabric strips needed to make curved appliqué stems and vines should be cut on the bias so that they are flexible enough to bend without wrinkles or puckers.

cutting bias strips

Strips for curved appliqué pattern pieces, such as meandering vines, and for binding curved edges should be cut on the bias, which runs at a 45° angle to the selvage of a woven fabric and has the most give or stretch.

To cut bias strips, begin with a fabric square or rectangle. Use a large acrylic ruler to square up the left edge of the fabric. Then make a cut at a 45° angle to the left edge (see Bias Strip Diagram, *above right*).

Handle the diagonal edges carefully to avoid distorting the bias. To cut a strip, measure the desired width parallel to the 45° cut edge; cut. Continue cutting enough strips to total the length needed.

Bias Strip Diagram

bias-bar method

This method uses metal or heat-resistant plastic bias bars purchased in sizes to match the desired finished width of each bias stem. If instructions for strip width and seam allowance are provided with your bias bars, refer to them. If not, refer to the following.

1. Cut a bias strip twice the desired finished width plus ¾". For example, for a ½"-wide finished bias stem, cut a 1¾"-wide bias strip. Handle the strip's edges carefully to prevent stretching. Fold the strip in half lengthwise with the wrong sides together; lightly press.

2. Stitch the length of the strip with the folded edge on the machine seam guide (to the right of the presser foot), the raw edges to the left, and a seam allowance equivalent to the desired finished width. For example, for a ½"-wide finished bias stem, stitch ½" away from the folded edge.

3. Trim away the seam allowance, leaving only enough fabric to hold the seam intact (about ¹⁄₁₆").

4. Slide the bias bar into the stem with the seam allowance centered on a flat side of the bar. Press the seam allowance to one side so that neither the seam nor the seam allowance is visible along the edges.

5. Remove the bar from the stem, and press the stem again.

6. Trace the stem placement line on the appliqué foundation fabric as a seam guide.

7. Pin the bias stem to the appliqué foundation covering the marked line and secure the stem in place using a machine blind-hem stitch or slip-stitching by hand.

finger-pressing method

1. Cut a bias strip to the desired finished width plus ½". For example, for a ¼"-wide finished bias stem, cut a ¾"-wide bias strip. Handle the strip's edges carefully to prevent stretching.

2. Finger-press under ¼" along both long edges.

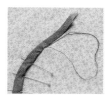

3. Pin the bias stem to the appliqué foundation and secure in place using a machine blind hem stitch or slip-stitching by hand.

fusible-web method

Using lightweight fusible web eliminates the need to turn under a strip's seam allowances. It is often the preferred method for making stems when the appliqués also are prepared with fusible web.

1. Cut a piece of lightweight fusible web the finished length of the desired stems by the width of a stem times the number of stems desired. For example, if you need 13 stems that are each ¼" wide and 10" long, cut a piece of fusible web to 3½×10". The extra ¼" allows you to make the first cut on the edge of the fusible web.

Cut a bias edge on your appliqué fabric. Following the manufacturer's directions, press the fusible-web piece to the wrong side of the appliqué fabric along the bias edge.

2. Trim the fabric to the edge of the fusible web. Then cut bias strips the desired finished widths and lengths of the appliqué stems.

3. Trace the stem placement line on the appliqué foundation fabric as a guide.

4. Peel off the paper backings. Following the manufacturer's directions, press the stems in place on the appliqué foundation, covering the marked line. Sew the bias stems to the appliqué foundation using a machine blind hem stitch or slip-stitching by hand.

position the appliqué pieces

There are many ways to position pieces for appliqué. Some require more preparation than others. If you're new to appliqué, experiment with different positioning methods to select the one that's best for you.

folded-foundation method

1. Cut the appliqué foundation fabric larger than the desired finished size to allow for any take-up in the fabric that might occur during the appliqué process. For example, for a 12" finished square, cut a 14"-square appliqué foundation. When the appliqué is complete, you'll trim the foundation to 12½" square. (The extra ¼" on each side will be used for seam allowances when assembling the quilt top.)

2. Fold the square appliqué foundation in half vertically and horizontally to find the center and divide the square into quarters. Lightly finger-press to create positioning guides for the appliqué pieces.

3. Fold the square appliqué foundation diagonally in both directions and lightly finger-press to make additional positioning guidelines.

4. Draw corresponding vertical, horizontal, and diagonal positioning guidelines on your full-size appliqué pattern if they are not already marked.

5. Prepare the appliqué pieces using the desired method. (See Prepare Appliqué Pieces beginning on *page 82.*) Referring to your appliqué pattern, pin and stitch the appliqué pieces to the foundation using your desired method; work from the bottom layer up.

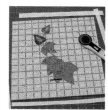

6. After the appliqué is complete, trim the appliqué foundation to the desired finished size plus seam allowances.

marked-foundation method

1. Cut the appliqué foundation fabric larger than the desired finished size to allow for any take-up in the fabric that might occur during the appliqué process. For example, for a 12" finished square, cut a 14"-square appliqué foundation. When the appliqué is complete, you'll trim the foundation square to 12½" square. (The extra ¼" on each side will be used for seam allowances when assembling the quilt top.)

2. Using a faint pencil line and your full-size appliqué pattern, trace the design onto the appliqué foundation fabric. To avoid having markings show after the appliqué is complete, lightly mark just inside the design lines and just at the critical points (for example, where two lines intersect or at the tips of leaves).

3. Prepare the appliqué pieces using the desired method. Referring to your appliqué pattern, pin and stitch the appliqué pieces to the foundation using your desired method; work from the bottom layer up.

4. After the appliqué is complete, trim the appliqué foundation to the desired size plus seam allowances.

light-box method

1. Cut the appliqué foundation fabric larger than the desired finished size to allow for any take-up in the fabric that might occur during the appliqué process. For example, for a 12" finished square, cut a 14"-square appliqué foundation. When the appliqué is complete, you'll trim the foundation square to 12½" square. (The extra ¼" on each side will be used for seam allowances when assembling the quilt top.)

2. Place your full-size appliqué pattern on a light box; secure it with tape. Center the appliqué foundation fabric atop the appliqué pattern.

3. Prepare the appliqué pieces using the desired method. (See Prepare Appliqué Pieces beginning on page 82.) Return to the light box and pin the bottom layer of the appliqué pieces in place on the appliqué foundation. Stitch the appliqué pieces to the foundation using your desired method.

4. After stitching the bottom layer of the appliqué pieces, return the appliqué foundation to the light box. Match the next layer of appliqué pieces with the pattern, pin, and stitch. Continue in this manner until all appliqué pieces are stitched to the foundation.

5. Trim the appliqué foundation to the desired size plus seam allowances.

overlay method

1. Cut the appliqué foundation fabric larger than the desired finished size to allow for any take-up in the fabric that might occur during the appliqué process. For example, for a 12" finished square, cut a 14"-square appliqué foundation. When the appliqué is complete, you'll trim the foundation square to 12½" square. (The extra ¼" on each side will be used for seam allowances when assembling the quilt top.)

2. Position clear upholstery vinyl (or other clear flexible plastic) over your full-size appliqué pattern and precisely trace the design with a permanent marker.

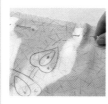

3. Center the vinyl overlay on the appliqué foundation fabric. Pin the top of the overlay to the foundation.

4. Prepare the appliqué pieces using the desired method. (See Prepare Appliqué Pieces beginning on page 82.) Once the appliqué pieces have been prepared, slide the bottommost appliqué piece right side up between the appliqué foundation and the overlay. When the piece is in place beneath its corresponding position on the vinyl overlay, remove the overlay and pin the appliqué piece to the foundation. Stitch the appliqué to the foundation using your desired method.

5. Pin the vinyl overlay on the foundation, and position the next appliqué piece in the stitching sequence. Pin and stitch it to the foundation as before. Continue adding appliqué pieces in this manner until all appliqués have been stitched in place.

6. Trim the appliqué foundation to the desired size plus seam allowances.

hold appliqué pieces in place

Once the appliqués and foundations have been prepared for stitching, the appliqué pieces can be held in place with pins, basting threads, spray adhesive, fabric glue or a glue stick, or fusible web. The number of appliqué layers you are working with may influence your choice.

PINS: Use as many straight pins as needed to hold each appliqué piece in place on the appliqué foundation for both machine and hand appliqué. Pins are generally used to hold no more than two layers at a time and are pushed through from the top. Some hand appliquérs like to place pins on the back side of the work to prevent catching thread in pins as they work. Remove the pins as you stitch.

BASTING: Sewing long stitches about ¼" from the turned-under edges is another way to secure prepared appliqué pieces to a foundation for both machine and hand appliqué. Begin and end the basting stitches on the right side of the appliqué for easier removal. You may wish to remove basting stitches when the entire appliqué work is complete or, if the basting threads impede stitching progress, remove them as you go. This is the preferred method for quilters who wish to hold multiple appliqué layers in position at once before permanently stitching them in place.

FABRIC BASTING SPRAY: When lightly sprayed on the wrong side of appliqué pieces, this adhesive usually allows you to position and reposition appliqués while you work. It can hold appliqués in place for both machine and hand appliqué. Work in a well-ventilated area and cover your work surface with paper. Be careful to spray lightly, as overspraying can cause a gummy buildup that makes stitching difficult.

FABRIC GLUE OR GLUE STICK: Apply these adhesives lightly to the wrong side of the prepared appliqué pieces along the outer edges or in the center. Press the appliqué piece to the appliqué foundation fabric. Be sure to apply the glue sparingly to avoid a buildup that would be difficult to stitch through. This method can be used for both machine and hand appliqué.

FUSIBLE WEB: This adhesive is most often used to hold pieces in position for machine appliqué. If you have an appliqué project with multiple layers of pieces that are prepared with fusible web, you may wish to hold them in position before adhering them to the foundation. To do so, place your full-size appliqué pattern beneath a clear, nonstick pressing sheet. Layer the prepared appliqué pieces in position right side up on the pressing sheet. Press lightly, just enough to fuse the pieces together, following the manufacturer's instructions. Do not slide the iron, but pick it up and move it from one area to the next. Let the pieces cool, then remove the fused appliqués from the pressing sheet and fuse them to the appliqué foundation.

machine appliqué
beginning and ending stitching

1. To begin stitching, bring the bobbin and needle threads to the top; this helps prevent thread tangles and snarls on the wrong side of your work. To begin this way, put the presser foot down and take one stitch. Stop and pull the bobbin thread to the top.

2. Set your machine for a narrow zigzag or satin stitch. Holding the bobbin and needle threads to one side, take a few stitches on a curve or straight edge; do not start at an inner or outer point. (If your machine has a variable stitch length, you may wish to set your stitch length at 0 and take a few stitches, one on top of the next, to lock threads in place at the start.) Reset your machine to the desired stitch setting; stitch about 1" and trim off the thread tails. Or when the appliqué work is completed, use a needle to draw the thread tails to the wrong side of the work and bury them in the stitching.

3. To end, stitch one or two threads past the point where the stitching began and take one or two backstitches to secure the thread. (If your machine has a variable stitch length, you may wish to set your stitch length at 0 and take a few stitches, one on top of the next, to lock the threads in place.)

satin- or zigzag-stitch appliqué

Variable-width satin or zigzag stitch makes a smooth, professional-looking finish on appliqué edges. Choose a thread color that complements or matches your appliqué fabric. Select a stitch width that corresponds to the size of the piece being appliquéd. Larger pieces can accommodate a wider, denser appliqué stitch than smaller appliqué shapes can.

ABOUT STABILIZERS

Stabilizers are used beneath appliqué foundations to add support and eliminate puckers and pulling on the fabric as you machine-appliqué. Some stabilizers are temporary and are removed once stitching is complete (as in the photo *left,* where the stabilizer is removed by holding it firmly on one side of the stitching and gently pulling it away from the other side). Others are permanent and remain in the quilt or are only partially cut away after stitching. Many brands are available. Two of the most common types are tear-away and water-soluble stabilizers. Freezer paper also may be used. Experiment with a variety of types to determine which works best for you.

With a machine satin stitch, it is not necessary to turn under the appliqué piece's edges because the entire outer edge is held in place by the zigzag or satin stitch. The outer edge of the stitch just grazes the appliqué foundation. Depending upon the stability of your fabric, the appliqué design, and your personal preference, you can use fusible web, pins, or fabric glue to hold the appliqué pieces in place for machine stitching. Use a stabilizer behind the appliqué foundation (see About Stabilizers on page 89).

1. Position the presser foot so that the left swing of the needle is on the appliqué and the right swing of the needle is just on the outer edge of the appliqué, grazing the appliqué foundation.

2. Begin stitching on a curve or straight edge, not at an inner or outer point.

pivoting at corners, curves, and points

The position of your needle is critical when pivoting fabric to round a curve or turn a point or corner. Use the following illustrations to guide you in knowing when to pivot. In each case, you will need to place your needle down in the fabric before pivoting. In each illustration the arrows indicate stitching direction and the dots mark where the needle should be down for pivoting.

TURNING CORNERS–METHOD 1
With this method the stitches cross over one another in the corners.

1. Stop with the needle down in the fabric on the right-hand swing of the needle.

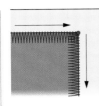

2. Raise the presser foot and pivot the fabric. Lower the presser foot and begin stitching to the next edge.

TURNING CORNERS–METHOD 2
With this method the stitching lines abut but do not cross over one another.

1. Stop with the needle down in the fabric on the left-hand swing of the needle.

2. Raise the presser foot and pivot the fabric. Lower the presser foot and turn the handwheel until the right-hand swing of the needle is just about to go into the foundation fabric. Lift the presser foot and reposition the foundation fabric so the tip of the needle is above the point where the needle thread is coming out of the appliqué. Lower the presser foot and begin stitching to the next edge.

PIVOTING INSIDE CURVES

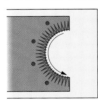

Stop at the first pivot point with the needle down in the fabric on the left-hand swing of the needle. Raise the presser foot, pivot the fabric slightly, and begin stitching to the next pivot point. Repeat as needed to round the entire inner curve.

PIVOTING OUTSIDE CURVES

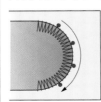

Stop at the first pivot point with the needle down in the fabric on the right-hand swing of the needle. Raise the presser foot, pivot the fabric slightly, and begin stitching to the next pivot point. Repeat as needed to round the entire outer curve.

PIVOTING INSIDE POINTS

1. With a marking tool, mark a line extending from the upcoming edge of the appliqué into the center. On the line, measure from the point a distance equal to your stitch width; mark the location with a dot.

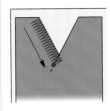

2. Stitch to the bottom of the inside point, stopping with the needle down in the fabric on the left-hand swing of the needle. The needle should be at the dot on your drawn marked line.

3. Raise the presser foot and pivot the fabric. Lower the presser foot and turn the handwheel until the right-hand swing of the needle is just about to go into the foundation fabric. Lift the presser foot and reposition the foundation fabric so the tip of the needle is above the point where the needle thread is coming out of the appliqué. Lower the presser foot and begin stitching to the next edge.

PIVOTING OUTSIDE POINTS
Shapes with outside points are among the more difficult to appliqué. This method requires you to taper your stitch width at the point. If your project requires you to appliqué around this shape, practice first on scraps to perfect your technique.

1. Stitch along the first edge of the appliqué, keeping the stitch width consistent until the left-hand swing of the needle begins to touch the opposite outside edge of the point. Stop with the needle down in the fabric on the left-hand swing of the needle.

2. Gradually reduce your stitch width and continue sewing toward the point. Keep the right- and left-hand swings of the needle just grazing the outer edges and taper your stitch width until it's 0 at the point. Stop with the needle down in the fabric.

3. Raise the presser foot and pivot the fabric. Lower the presser foot and begin stitching away from the point, increasing the stitch width at the same rate that you decreased it until you have returned to the original stitch width. Pivot the fabric slightly as needed to keep the right-hand swing of the needle grazing the foundation at the right-hand edge of the appliqué piece.

mock hand appliqué

This method uses monofilament thread in the needle and the blind-hem stitch to make virtually invisible stitches. ***Note:*** Contrasting thread was used in the photos that follow for illustration purposes only.

1. Prepare the appliqué pieces following Freezer-Paper Method 3 on page 84.

2. Position an appliqué piece so that the needle goes into the appliqué foundation right next to it. The needle should be so near the fold of the appliqué piece that it touches the fold but does not stitch through it.

When the needle jumps to the left, the stitch should be totally on the appliqué piece.

When the needle jumps to the right to complete a zigzag stitch, the needle should again be against the edge of the appliqué piece but go through the foundation only.

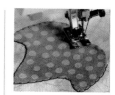

3. When you come to inside and outside points, make sure to secure them with several stitches. Make certain the needle always touches the fold of the appliqué so no edges are missed.

4. Continue stitching around the appliqué. When you reach the location where the stitching began, stitch over the beginning stitches to secure the threads. To lock your stitches, backstitch only two or three stitches.

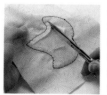

5. When the stitching is complete, check all the edges of the appliqué to make sure no areas were left unstitched. On the wrong side, carefully trim away the foundation fabric from within each stitched shape, leaving a ¼" seam allowance.

6. Using a spritzer bottle, spray water on the inside of the appliqué's seam allowances, making sure to wet the areas that were glued over the freezer paper.

MACHINE APPLIQUÉ TROUBLESHOOTING TIPS

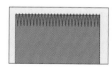

THIS MACHINE-APPLIQUÉ STITCHING IS CORRECTLY PLACED. The outside edge of the stitch is just grazing the appliqué foundation.

THIS STITCHING IS TOO FAR INSIDE the edge of the appliqué piece, so fabric threads from the appliqué will fray and poke out around the edges.

HERE THE STITCHES ARE TOO FAR OUTSIDE the edge of the appliqué piece, so it may pull loose from the foundation.

GAPS WILL OCCUR in the stitching if your needle is down in the fabric on the wrong side of the needle swing when you pivot.

YOUR STITCHES WILL SLANT if you try to pull or push the fabric through curves, rather than lifting the presser foot and pivoting the fabric.

PIVOTING TOO SOON on an inside point will leave an incomplete line of stitches at the point.

MOCK HAND APPLIQUÉ TROUBLESHOOTING TIPS:

- If your stitching shows, you may be stitching too far from the edge of the appliqué. If you miss stitching into the appliqué with the zigzag, the stitches will be visible.
- If there are gaps in your stitching, the stitch length may be too long.
- If you see too much of the zigzag stitch, its width is too big.

7. Remove the paper. You'll find that once the water dissolves the glue, the freezer paper will slip right out.

SEWING MACHINE SETUP FOR MOCK HAND APPLIQUÉ

- Make certain your machine is clean and in good working order.
- Install a new size 60/8, 70/10, or 75/11 embroidery needle in your machine.
- Wind a bobbin with cotton 60-weight embroidery thread.
- Thread the needle with lightweight, invisible, nylon (monofilament) thread. Use clear thread for light-color fabrics; use smoke-color invisible thread for medium- and dark-color fabrics.
- Set your machine for a blind hem stitch with the stitch width and length each set at 1mm. This stitch takes 2 to 5 straight stitches, then a zigzag, then 2 to 5 more straight stitches before zigzagging again.

Stitch a test sample using the same threads and fabrics as those in your project.

The distance between each zigzag should be ⅛" maximum, and the zigzag width should be the width of two threads. When you are finished, you should be able to see the needle holes but no thread. If you gently pull on the edge of the appliqué, the stitching should be strong and without gaps.

Check the stitch tension on the test sample. There should be no bobbin thread showing on the top and no loops of nylon thread on the bottom. If the bobbin thread is showing on the top, loosen the top tension gradually until the bobbin thread no longer shows. Turn the sample over. If there are loops of nylon thread on the bottom, you've loosened the top tension too much.

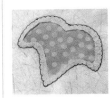

8. When the freezer paper has been removed from all appliqués, place a thick bath towel atop your pressing surface and lay the appliqué facedown on the towel. Cover the back of appliqué with a pressing cloth; press with a warm iron. (The towel prevents edges of the appliqués from being flattened by the iron.) *Note:* Contrasting thread is used here for illustration purposes only. If monofilament thread had been used, no stitching line would be visible on the right side of the fabric.

straight-stitch appliqué

1. Prepare the appliqué pieces following the desired method. (For more information, see Prepare Appliqué Pieces beginning on page 82) Pin, baste, or glue the appliqués in place.

2. Set the stitch length at 0. Beginning on a straight edge or a curve, take two or three stitches about ⅛" from the outer edge of the appliqué to anchor the thread. Hold the thread tails out of the way to prevent thread snarls on the underside. *Note:* Remove pins before the needle reaches them.

3. Adjust the stitch length to the desired number of stitches per inch (12 to 15) and continue sewing around the appliqué edge, staying ⅛" from the outer edge.

4. To stitch inner and outer curves, stop with the needle down, lift the presser foot, pivot the appliqué foundation, lower the presser foot, and continue sewing.

5. To end your stitching, gradually reduce the stitch length to 0 as you meet the point where the stitching began. Make the last two or three stitches next to the stitches where you started. Do not backstitch or overlap stitches.

Note: Contrasting thread was used in the photographs for illustration purposes only. In the photograph, monofilament thread was used on the sample so the stitching line does not appear as visible on the right side of the appliqué.

SEWING MACHINE SETUP FOR STRAIGHT-STITCH APPLIQUÉ

- Make certain your machine is clean and in good working order.
- Install a new size 60/8, 70/10, 75/11, or 80/12 sharp embroidery needle in your machine.
- Wind a bobbin with cotton 60-weight embroidery thread.
- Thread the needle with thread in a color that matches the appliqué or a lightweight, invisible nylon (monofilament) thread.
- Set your machine for a straight stitch with the stitch length at 12 to 15 stitches per inch.

Stitch a test sample using the same thread and fabrics as your project. If your tension is properly adjusted, no bobbin thread will show on the top of your appliqué.

TIP: For machine appliqué, use a 60/8, 70/10, 75/11, or 80/12 sharp needle. For best results, use a smaller number needle for lighter weight, finer fabrics, and monofilament threads; use a larger number needle for medium-weight fabrics and cotton threads. Sewing on flannel or working with decorative threads requires larger or specialty needles.

decorative-stitch appliqué

This technique is often done on a sewing machine using the blanket or buttonhole stitch. Other decorative stitches also may be used, such as the featherstitch.

1. Prepare the appliqué pieces following the desired method. (For more information, see Prepare Appliqué Pieces beginning on page 82.) Pin, baste, or glue the appliqués in place.

2. Use a tear-away stabilizer beneath the appliqué foundation. (See About Stabilizers on page 89.)

3. Beginning on a straight edge or a curve, take a few stitches; hold the thread tails out of the way to prevent thread snarls on the wrong side of your project. The right swing of the needle should graze the appliqué foundation. The left swing of the needle should be completely on the appliqué piece.

4. For inside curves, stop with the needle down in the fabric on the left needle swing, lift the presser foot, pivot the appliqué foundation, lower the presser foot, and continue sewing.

5. For outside curves, stop with the needle down in the fabric on the right needle swing, lift the presser foot, pivot the appliqué foundation, and then continue sewing.

6. Adjust the stitch length as necessary at corners and where the stitching meets at the end.

TIP: To produce uniform stitches when doing machine appliqué, work slowly and sew at an even pace.

fusible-web appliqué

To finish the edges of appliqué pieces that have been fused to the appliqué foundation, follow the instructions for Satin- or Zigzag-Stitch Appliqué, which begin on page 89 or Decorative Stitch Appliqué on this page. Be sure you have prepared your appliqués with a sew-through fusible web. (See Prepare Appliqué Pieces—Fusible-Web Method beginning on page 87.)

TIP: Manufacturer's instructions for adhering fusible web vary by brand. Follow the instructions that come with your fusible web to ensure success. Factors such as the iron's temperature setting, a dry or steam iron, and the length of time you press are critical to attaining a secure bond between the fusible web and fabric.

wool appliqué

Felted wool—wool that has been napped and shrunk—is easy to work with because the edges will not ravel so there is no need to turn them under. Use templates to cut felted wool into appliqué pieces. Do not include seam allowances. (See Making Appliqué Templates, which begins on page 82.)

Use a basic running stitch or decorative hand- or machine-embroidery stitches to attach wool appliqués to an appliqué foundation. Or, for added dimension, tack wool appliqué pieces at their centers only. To felt wool for use in appliqué, machine-wash it in a hot-water/cool-rinse cycle with a small amount of detergent, machine-dry, and steam-press. It is the disparity in temperatures, along with the agitation, that causes the wool to felt. If you wish to use wool from a piece of clothing, cut it apart and remove the seams so it can shrink freely.

quilting basics

Read through these general quilting instructions to ensure you'll properly cut and assemble your quilt. Accuracy in each step guarantees a successful quiltmaking experience.

getting started
BASIC TOOLS

Acrylic ruler: To aid in making perfectly straight cuts with a rotary cutter, choose a ruler of thick, clear plastic. Many sizes are available. A 6×24" ruler marked in ¼" increments with 30°, 45°, and 60° angles is a good first purchase.

Rotary-cutting mat: A rotary cutter should always be used with a mat designed specifically for it. In addition to protecting the table, the mat helps keep the fabric from shifting while you cut. Often these mats are described as self-healing, meaning the blade does not leave slash marks or grooves in the surface, even after repeated usage.

Rotary cutter: The round blade of a rotary cutter will cut up to six layers of fabric at once. Because the blade is so sharp, be sure to purchase one with a safety guard and keep the guard over the blade when you're not cutting. The blade can be removed from the handle and replaced when it gets dull.

Scissors: You'll need one pair for cutting fabric and another for cutting paper and plastic.

Pencils and other marking tools: Marks made with special quilt markers are easy to remove after sewing.

Template plastic: This slightly frosted plastic comes in sheets about ¹⁄₁₆" thick.

Iron and ironing board: Pressing the seams ensures accurate piecing.

Sewing thread: Use 100% cotton thread.

Sewing machine: Any machine in good working order with well-adjusted tension will produce pucker-free patchwork seams.

HAND QUILTING

Frame or hoop: You'll get smaller, more even stitches if you stretch your quilt as you stitch. A frame supports the quilt's weight, ensures even tension, and frees both your hands for stitching. However, once set up, it cannot be disassembled until the quilting is complete. Quilting hoops are more portable and less expensive.

Quilting needles: A "between" or quilting needle is short with a small eye. Common sizes are 8, 9, and 10; size 8 is best for beginners.

Quilting thread: Quilting thread is stronger than sewing thread.

Thimble: This finger cover relieves the pressure required to push a needle through several layers of fabric and batting.

MACHINE QUILTING

Darning foot: You may find this tool, also called a hopper foot, in your sewing machine's accessory kit. If not, have the model and brand of your machine available when you go to purchase one. It is used for free-motion stitching.

Safety pins: They hold the layers together during quilting.

Table: Use a large work surface that's level with your machine bed.

Thread: Use 100% cotton quilting thread, cotton-wrapped polyester quilting thread, or fine nylon monofilament thread.

Walking foot: This sewing-machine accessory helps you keep long, straight quilting lines smooth and pucker-free.

CHOOSE YOUR FABRICS

It is no surprise that most quilters prefer 100% cotton fabrics for quiltmaking. Cotton fabric minimizes seam distortion, presses crisply, and is easy to quilt. Most patterns, including those in this book, specify quantities for 44/45"-wide fabrics unless otherwise noted. Our projects call for a little extra yardage in length to allow for minor errors and slight shrinkage.

PREPARE YOUR FABRICS

There are conflicting opinions about the need to prewash fabric. The debate is a modern one because most antique quilts were made with unwashed fabric. However, the dyes and sizing used today are unlike those used a century ago.

Prewashing fabric offers quilters certainty as its main advantage. Today's fabrics resist bleeding and shrinkage, but some of both can occur in some fabrics—an unpleasant prospect once you've assembled a quilt. Some quilters find prewashed fabric easier to quilt. If you choose to prewash your fabric, press it well before cutting.

Other quilters prefer the crispness of unwashed fabric, especially for machine piecing. And, if you use fabrics with the same fiber content throughout a quilt, then any shrinkage that occurs in its first washing should be uniform. Some quilters find this small amount of shrinkage desirable because it gives a quilt a slightly puckered, antique look.

We recommend you prewash a scrap of each fabric to test it for shrinkage and bleeding. If you choose to prewash an entire fabric piece, unfold it to a single layer. Wash it in warm water to allow the fabric to shrink and/or bleed. If the fabric bleeds, rinse it until the water runs clear. Do not use it in a quilt if it hasn't stopped bleeding. Hang the fabric to dry, or tumble it in the dryer until slightly damp; press well.

finishing
LAYERING

Cut and piece the backing fabric to measure at least 3" longer on all sides than the quilt top. Press all seam allowances open. With wrong sides together, layer the quilt top and backing fabric with the batting in between; baste. Quilt as desired.

BINDING

The binding for most quilts is cut on the straight grain of the fabric. If your quilt has curved edges, cut the strips on the bias (see Appliqué Primer, which begins on *page 84*). The cutting instructions for projects in this book specify the number of binding strips or a total length needed to finish the quilt. The instructions also specify enough width for a French-fold, or double-layer, binding because it's easier to apply and adds durability.

Join the strips with diagonal seams to make one continuous binding strip (see Diagram 1, *above, left*). Trim the excess fabric, leaving ¼" seam allowances. Press seam allowances open. Then, with the wrong sides together, fold under 1" at one end of the binding strip (see Diagram 2, *above, top right*); press. Fold the strip in half lengthwise (see Diagram 3, *above, bottom right*); press.

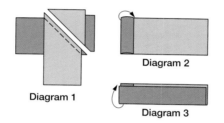

Diagram 1

Diagram 2

Diagram 3

Beginning in the center of one side, place the binding strip against the right side of the quilt top, aligning the binding strip's raw edges with the quilt top's raw edge (see Diagram 4, *right*). Beginning 1½" from the folded edge, sew through all layers, stopping ¼" from the corner. Backstitch, then clip the threads. Remove the quilt from under the sewing-machine presser foot.

Fold the binding strip upward (see Diagram 5, *right*), creating a diagonal fold, and finger-press.

Holding the diagonal fold in place with your finger, bring the binding strip down in line with the next edge, making a horizontal fold that aligns with the first edge of the quilt (see Diagram 6, *right*).

Start sewing again at the top of the horizontal fold, stitching through all layers. Sew around the quilt, turning each corner in the same manner.

When you return to the starting point, lap the binding strip inside the beginning fold (see Diagram 7, *right*). Finish sewing to the starting point (see Diagram 8, *right*). Trim the batting and backing fabric even with the quilt top edges.

Turn the binding over the edge of the quilt to the back. Hand-stitch the binding to the backing fabric, making sure to cover any machine stitching.

To make mitered corners on the back, hand-stitch the binding up to a corner; fold a miter in the binding. Take a stitch or two in the fold to secure it. Then stitch the binding in place up to the next corner. Finish each corner in the same manner.

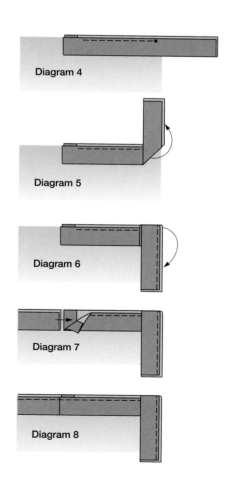

Diagram 4

Diagram 5

Diagram 6

Diagram 7

Diagram 8

Better Homes and Gardens®
Creative Collection™

Editorial Director
Gayle Goodson Butler

Editor-in-Chief
Beverly Rivers

Executive Editor	Karman Wittry Hotchkiss
Contributing Editorial Manager	Heidi Palkovic
Contributing Design Director	Tracy DeVenney
Contributing Graphic Designer	Kim Hopkins
Contributing Copy Editor	Lisa Flyr
Contributing Proofreaders	Joleen Ross
	Dana Schmidt
Copy Chief	Mary Heaton
Administrative Assistant	Lori Eggers

Senior Vice President
Bob Mate

Publishing Group President
Jack Griffin

Chairman and CEO	William T. Kerr
President and COO	Stephen M. Lacy

In Memoriam
E. T. Meredith III (1933–2003)